Intrusion Detection Honeypots

Detection through Deception

by Chris Sanders

Publisher: Chris Sanders
Cover Design: Bailey McGinn
Interior Design: Susan Veach
Copy Editor: Amanda Robinson
Proofreader: Johanna Petronella Leigh
Technical Editors: Josh Brower, David Bianco, Marco Slaviero
Indexer: Cheryl Lenser

ISBN-13: 978-1-7351883-0-0 (Paperback)
ISBN-13: 978-1-7351883-1-7 (ePub)

Library of Congress Cataloging-in-Publication Application Submitted

For information on distribution, translations, or bulk sales, please contact Chris Sanders directly.
Applied Network Defense
PO Box 52
Oakwood, GA 30566
chris@appliednetworkdefense.com

This book is dedicated to public school teachers.
Make time today to thank one who impacted your life.

Brief Content

Detailed Content

Acknowledgments

Although it's my name alone on this book's spine, it would not appear there if not for the support of many others. I'd like to take this opportunity to thank those who supported the production of Intrusion Detection Honeypots or who supported me while writing it.

First and foremost, a heartfelt thank you to my wife, Ellen. Your support during this process and your help managing the cognitive load of the household were priceless.

I've been fortunate to work with many incredibly talented people who see the world in unique, interesting ways. While there are far too many to name, I want to extend special thanks to Alek Rollyson, Stef Rand, and Jason Smith for providing their thoughts on various components of this book and serving as sounding boards.

While researching this book, I spoke to dozens of people who helped provide valuable perspectives. Thank you to Ross Bevington, Haroon Meer, Lance Spitzner, and several others who directly or indirectly helped shape the content of this book.

Although I've written several other books, this title is my first venture into self-publishing. I knew that assembling a top-notch team would make all the difference, and it has. Thank you to my copy editor Amanda Robinson and proofreader Johanna Leigh for helping things make more sense. Thank you to my technical editors Josh Brower, David Bianco, and Marco Slaviero for validating concepts and providing different perspectives. Thank you to Michael W. Lucas for providing guidance on the independent publishing process. Thank you to Stacy Edwards for helping with some of the graphics, Bailey McGinn for her beautiful cover design, Cheryl Lenser for her indexing work, and Susan Veach for designing the inside of the book and setting the text.

Finally, thank you to public school teachers. The ones who impacted me, and all the rest of them too. They are important and don't get paid enough.

This book was written to the soundtrack of fellow Kentucky native, Tyler Childers.

About the Author

Chris Sanders is a computer security analyst, educator, and researcher.

He is the founder of Applied Network Defense, a company focused on delivering high quality, accessible information security training. In previous roles, Chris worked with the US Department of Defense, InGuardians, and Mandiant building security operation centers and training security practitioners focused on defending networks.

Chris is also the founder and director of the Rural Technology Fund, a non-profit that donates instructional resources to public schools to further STEM education in rural and high poverty areas. To date, the RTF has put computer science education resources into the hands of over 100,000 students in all 50 states.

Chris has authored numerous books and articles, including the international bestseller *Practical Packet Analysis* from No Starch Press, currently in its third edition and in seven languages, and *Applied Network Security Monitoring* from Syngress. His current research focuses on the intersection of cyber security and cognitive psychology, with the goal of enhancing the field of infosec investigative disciplines through a better understanding of the human thought and learning processes. He hopes to complete his Doctorate of Education from Baylor in the Fall of 2021.

Chris blogs at http://www.chrissanders.org and tweets @chrissanders88. You can learn more about Applied Network Defense at http://www.networkdefense.co and the RTF at http://www.ruraltechfund.org.

"It's a trap!"
- Admiral Ackbar

INTRODUCTION

MY COMPUTER SCIENCE PROFESSORS WOULD
probably be horrified to know that the scholarly quote that stuck with
me the most from my undergraduate education came from my World
Civilization class:

> *"If you want to understand the world of nature, learn physics. If you want to understand the world of humankind, learn economics."*

I'll leave the physics to someone else, but you can't spend much time working in
information security without acknowledging that economics drives its human-centric
existence. We protect information because it has some financial or social value. Threats
to the confidentiality, integrity, or availability of that data represent a risk to that value, so
we spend money to protect it. Ideally, the cost of protection is less than the value of what
we're protecting, or else we've created an unfavorable imbalance.

Despite the industry's mediocre ability to calculate the value of data, the cost to
defend networks has grown dramatically. If you were to characterize the history of
computer network defense over the past thirty years in a conversation, it might go like this
. . .

Business: Someone broke into my system!
Security Industry: Buy a firewall.

Business: A user got a virus!
Security Industry: Buy antivirus software.

Business: My AV missed something!
Security Industry: Buy a network intrusion detection system.

Business: My IDS doesn't provide enough alert context!
Security Industry: Buy centralized logging.

Business: The number of logs and alerts are overwhelming and challenging to manage!
Security Industry: Buy a Security Incident and Event Monitoring (SIEM) console.

Business: I'm still missing important security events!
Security Industry: Buy access to a threat intelligence feed.

Business: I've got way too many IDS and AV alerts to investigate!
Security Industry: Buy a Managed Security Service Provider (MSSP) contract.

Business: I'm still missing attacks!
Security Industry: Buy a machine learning tool.

Business: All this stuff is time-consuming to manage!
Security Industry: Hire more security people.

As the security industry trumpets the adoption of more numerous and complex defensive tech products, the cost for consumers increases prohibitively. While this might be palatable to governments and large organizations, everyone else gets left behind. In the US alone, the Department of Labor classifies approximately 90% of all businesses as small businesses with less than 50 employees. How many of these can afford to purchase or employ staff to support even half of the things from the conversation above?

Even worse, consider industries that don't have significant financial resources by virtue of the areas they focus on, such as public schools, nonprofits, human service organizations, and smaller city and county governments. Many of these groups rely on external providers for essential IT support and can't afford to hire dedicated system or network administrators, let alone anyone dedicated to security. In the infosec bubble, it's easy to forget that security is still a specialized service that most can't afford. While information security providers were busy trying to figure out how to scale up, they forgot the importance of scaling down complexity and costs so that security is available to everyone who needs it.

It's in the spirit of attainable and equitable access to information security that I present this book.

While I can't tackle the full breadth of the broader economic imbalances I've described, I do hope that by focusing on a particular facet of the security landscape, I'll be able to help your organization save some money and uncover more evil. After all, I'm not an economist. I'm an analyst, and it's my job to build a better mousetrap, one that can be used to catch the people who seek to steal data that doesn't belong to them[1]. This book describes the theory and use of my favorite mousetrap, honeypots.

An *Intrusion Detection Honeypot* (IDH) is a security resource placed inside your network perimeter that generates alerts when probed, attacked, or compromised. These systems, services, or tokens rely on deception to lure attackers in and convince them to interact. Unbeknownst to the attacker, you're alerted when that interaction occurs and can begin investigating the compromise. This approach lends itself to intrusion detection with a low false-positive rate and minimal maintenance overhead, lowering your cost to defend data. The method is also extensible, allowing you to configure increased interaction levels that help discern your attacker's tradecraft and goals.

I first wrote about intrusion detection honeypots in a dedicated chapter of my 2013 book, *Applied Network Security Monitoring*. While the concept wasn't entirely new, it was clear at the time that most only thought of honeypots as research tools rather than as having a functional place in their organization's network security monitoring strategy. That has somewhat changed since 2013 as more people have embraced detection honeypots through the development of custom-written scripts, free and open source tools, and commercial product offerings. I'm excited to see this. While not a panacea, I believe honeypot-based detection represents one of the best investments many organizations can make for detecting compromise.

My goal with *Intrusion Detection Honeypots* is to convince you that IDH technology has a place in your network and can equip you with the tools and knowledge you'll need to be successful in designing, implementing and monitoring it.

Audience and Prerequisites

I wrote this book for practicing analysts, investigators, sysadmins, net admins, detection engineers, or anyone else seeking to expand their detection capabilities with new and

---

[1] Or as I like to tell my non-techie friends, I'm like Batman, but on the internet.

effective techniques. It assumes some basic understanding of systems, networks, and security concepts.

Building and tuning detection is one function of the security specialty known as *Network Security Monitoring* (NSM), which is the collection, detection, and analysis of network security data to find and investigate intrusions. This book assumes some basic understanding and experience with NSM. If you'd like to get up to speed in that area, I recommend the following two books:

Applied Network Security Monitoring: Collection, Detection, and Analysis by Chris Sanders and Jason Smith (2013)

The Practice of Network Security Monitoring: Understanding Incident Detection and Response by Richard Bejtlich (2013)

Additionally, the following book provides a reasonable overview of the incident handling process:

Incident Response & Computer Forensics by Jason Luttgens, Matthew Pepe, and Kevin Mandia (2014)

Encapsulated among those books, and at the core of NSM, are three main assumptions we'll work from:

Prevention Eventually Fails

No matter how deliberate your efforts, an attacker who is relentlessly motivated or resourced will eventually gain access to a device on your network. Therefore, you should deploy detection mechanisms to aid in investigating and responding to attacks as quickly as possible.

You Don't Lose When the Attacker Gets In

The attacker's goal isn't merely to gain access to a device on your network. Attackers have objectives, and defenders typically don't lose until an attacker accomplishes one or more of them. You don't lose when one of your users clicks a link in a phishing e-mail or when an attacker harvests VPN credentials with drive-by malware. You lose when an attacker exfiltrates intellectual property or scrapes thousands of credit card numbers from memory on point of sale terminals. Fortunately, these goals take time. It's in that particular space between initial access and completed objectives where you have the most significant opportunity for detection and response before the attacker causes substantial damage.

Humans Are at the Center of the Investigation

All the computers in the world combined can't match the abstract reasoning and fluid intelligence of the human brain that each of us possesses. While machines are great at automating things like data retrieval, it is humans who ultimately make decisions based on that data. Engineers should design security systems and their outputs with human analysts in mind.

Concepts and Approach

I intend for this book to strike a balance between the theory necessary to understand deception-based detection and the practical skills required to implement and maintain it. The first two chapters set the stage by defining honeypots and discussing their history. Following this, I describe frameworks for designing and planning honeypot detection and how these fit into the monitoring infrastructure supporting them. I devote the remaining chapters to specific honeypot deployment use cases.

While honeypots themselves are often simple, they exist in complex network ecosystems. As such, every use case scenario I describe might require adjustment for your particular needs. Although I've tried to write about widely applicable methods, keep in mind that I can't cover every potential scenario or edge case. Although I may cite something as best practice, this book ultimately constitutes theories based on my own research, experience, and opinions.

This book focuses entirely on free and open source tools. I did this not only to appeal to a larger group of individuals who may not have the funding to purchase commercial detection tools, but also to show the intrinsic benefit of using analyst-designed tools that provide more transparency into how they interact with data.

Intrusion Detection Honeypots was written with a flowing narrative in mind and is intended to be read from cover to cover while also serving as reference material once you begin to apply the content to your network or lab.

Chapter 1: A Brief History of Honeypots

The first chapter takes you through the history of honeypots, starting in the 1980s. I'll discuss landmarks in honeypot usage, such as Cliff Stoll's SDINet, Bill Cheswick's "Evening with Berferd," and the formation of the honeynet project.

Chapter 2: Defining and Classifying Honeypots

Because I've seen honeypots used in so many ways, this chapter seeks to describe the characteristics of honeypots and their common goals. I'll also discuss a framework for deceptive thinking and dispel traditional honeypot myths to make a more direct case for detection honeypots in every network.

Chapter 3: Planning Honeypot-Based Detection

This chapter introduces the See-Think-Do deception framework for planning honeypot-based detection deployment. I'll help you figure out what honeypots to build and where to deploy them.

Chapter 4: Logging and Monitoring

This chapter describes how to fit honeypots into your existing logging and monitoring infrastructure so that you'll know when attackers interact with them. I'll also cover some common tools and best practices for monitoring honeypots.

Chapter 5: Building Your First Honeypot from Scratch

Now that you understand the theory, it's time to get your hands dirty. I'll walk you through creating a simple honeypot using netcat.

Chapter 6: Honey Services

This chapter walks you through creating multiple honey services using a variety of techniques. These techniques include mimicking the RDP service with Windows, the SSH service with Cowrie, and various services with OpenCanary.

Chapter 7: Honey Tokens

Honey tokens are my favorite form of IDH, and I'll show you why in this chapter. You'll learn to create honeydocs from office files, other forms of honey files, and honey folders.

Chapter 8: Honey Credentials

Attackers often rely on credential theft to accomplish their goals, so this chapter shows you how to use that against them by deploying honey credentials to strategic network locations. I'll show you how to create honey token services, place honey credentials in memory, and deploy honey broadcasts.

Chapter 9: Unconventional Honeypots

In my research for this book, I encountered several unique use cases for detection honeypots. This chapter covers many of these unconventional techniques, including some that don't fit into a specific category, span multiple categories, or were just good ol' fashioned fun! I'll show you how to create DHCP honey services, honey tokens to detect website cloning, honey tables, honey mailboxes, and honey commands.

Technology Use

I provide several walkthroughs and examples used to configure honeypots and their supporting infrastructure. Unless otherwise specified, those instructions were written and tested using the following operating systems:

- Windows – Windows 10 Enterprise, Version 1903
- Linux – Ubuntu Linux 18.04 Server

Downloadable Resources

I provide scripts or configuration files not available elsewhere in multiple places throughout this book. Where appropriate, I've made this information available online in a GitHub repository at https://github.com/chrissanders/idh to save you some typing.

From the Trenches

Starting with Chapter 5, each chapter includes a "From the Trenches" section. These sidebars are stories that came from my research while writing this book. Each one represents the real experiences of practitioners who deployed some form of intrusion detection honeypots.

Charitable Support

I'm proud to donate a portion of the proceeds from this book to several charitable causes. By purchasing this book you've helped support:

- Donations to poverty-stricken classrooms to help teach students about computer science through the Rural Tech Fund (ruraltechfund.org).
- The purchase of mosquito nets to help save lives in underdeveloped countries through the Against Malaria Foundation (againstmalaria.org).
- Direct cash donations to individuals living in poverty through GiveDirectly (givedirectly.org).
- The construction of affordable homes for families in need through Habitat for Humanity (habitat.org).
- Feeding the hungry through several local food banks.

I believe that our lives, in the end, will be a verdict on our recognition of the extraordinary obligations which accompany extraordinary resources. Thank you for purchasing this book and helping us both fulfill that obligation.

Contact Me

I've put a tremendous amount of effort into researching and writing this book, so I'm always excited to hear from people who enjoy it or have thoughts to share. If you would like to contact me, you can send all questions, comments, threats, and marriage proposals directly to me at the following locations:

Chris Sanders
E-Mail: chris@chrissanders.org
Blog: https://chrissanders.org
Twitter: @chrissanders88
LinkedIn: https://www.linkedin.com/in/chrissanders88/

Aside from writing books like this one, my day job focuses on teaching people to be better security practitioners. I do that primarily through online courses through my company Applied Network Defense. If you like this book, then you'll probably like my classes too[2]. You can view my online course catalog at https://networkdefense.co.

A Final Note

My goal for this book is to convince you that honeypots are more than just research vessels and to also show you how you can use them as one of the highest-efficacy intrusion detection techniques in your tool belt. But, know that this book is a launching off point. The beautiful thing about deception and honeypots is that there are so many things you can do with them. In my research, I've encountered over a hundred unique honeypot deployment techniques successfully finding evil in real networks, but I've only covered a dozen or so of the most common in this text. There is much more for you to explore.

We all have curiosity inside of us, but it doesn't grow on its own . . . you have to feed it. May this book whet your appetite. Speaking of which, see Appendix A for something else that might . . .

---

[2] Imagine someone reading this book out loud to you dramatically, but with demonstrations and an appealing southern accent.

A BRIEF HISTORY OF HONEYPOTS

1

THE TERM HONEYPOT HAS A RICH AND DIVERSE history filled with people and stories that shaped information security. This history scaffolds the body of knowledge whose foundation we build upon, even today. Because the majority of people only have exposure to a small portion of that history, perceptions about what honeypots are and how they're used can vary wildly.

I've run the gamut of experiences throughout my career when attempting to deploy detection honeypots. Early on, I proposed detection honeypots while working for the US Army in a group that was known for being conservative in their approach. They laughed at me and told me to go back to working on IDS signatures. A few years later, I worked in an audit-heavy US Navy group. When I proposed detection honeypots to them, they told me to go ahead—but they were worried auditors would fly off the handle at the mention of honeypots and insisted I call them "sponges" in any official documentation. Years after that, while in a consulting role, I pitched a honeypot deployment to a Fortune 500 CISO who simply said, "Why haven't we done that already?"

In each case, these groups had strong opinions on what honeypots were, what value they provided, and the risk they represented. However, their perspectives were primarily framed around their first introduction to the topic. Some became excited when they saw the potential for low-cost, high-efficacy detection. Others experienced a visceral sensation as they envisioned rogue sysadmins inviting attackers to operate within shouting distance of their most critical assets.

Because people base so much of their opinions about honeypots on the history they know, I think it's best to begin with an overview of honeypot history. In this chapter, we'll talk about some early uses of honeypots and how they evolved over the past thirty years. I hope that, armed with this knowledge, you can enter conversations with decision-makers who might be opposed to honeypot deployment and win them over by anchoring to their known history and supplementing it with a broader perspective.

The Evolution of Honeypots

Honeypot history is interesting because people haven't primarily used honeypots in the spirit in which they were conceived. The first honeypots served a practical use, either detecting when an intruder attempted to gain access to a network or as a means of placing an actual human behind the keyboard as the source of an attack. The technology supporting these efforts was often custom-written and entirely specific to individual networks. Eventually, the threats of the time would push researchers to move toward research honeypots that were placed outside the network and were designed to track the proliferation of automated attacks and the actions of opportunistic attackers.

While this shift served the needs of the time, it took over a decade for the pendulum to start swinging back to the roots of honeypot technology as an effective means of detection and network security monitoring. I want to highlight a few critical moments in history that further illustrate these shifts.

The Cuckoo's Egg

In the late 1980s, an astronomer at Lawrence Berkeley Laboratory (LBL) in California named Cliff Stoll was tasked with helping maintain the school's computer network. This was a time when universities would purchase room-sized computers and charge for access to them to subsidize the massive cost. During a routine review of the accounting software that kept track of the computer usage, Cliff noticed 75 cents worth of computer time was missing. Someone used the time, but Cliff couldn't attribute it to one specific user.

As Cliff started to pull at this thread, a much larger picture began to unravel. The LBL network was under attack. For the next several months Cliff became an early pioneer of intrusion detection systems, setting up alerts when the attacker connected to his network. He also became one of the first people to utilize network security monitoring techniques to log the commands the attacker executed, allowing for a closer look at their tradecraft. Using these methods, he observed the attackers breaking in repeatedly, using exploits against popular software, and modifying system programs to include password stealing techniques. Eventually, the attackers used the LBL network as a pivot point to breach a long list of US government and military targets.

Cliff became obsessed with identifying whoever was behind these attacks. At the time, people accessed the Internet by phone line. Cliff interfaced with various phone companies to trace the calls made by the attackers into the network, enumerating their path back to its source one hop at a time. Eventually, they traced the attacker back to Germany before the process hit a roadblock. The local switching station the attacker dialed from was antiquated, and to associate the call with a specific line would require an on-site technician performing a physical trace. Mapping the connection could take a couple of hours, but the attacker's sessions typically weren't that long. So, Cliff had to figure out how to lure the attacker into staying on the network for an extended period.

This problem brings us to one of the first documented honeypot uses. Cliff observed the type of data the attacker had been searching for. So, with an idea inspired by his girlfriend Martha, he decided to give it to them. He devised a fake missile defense project named SDINET and painstakingly drafted a trove of false documents to make it look like the real deal. Cliff placed the materials on a system the attacker had access to in a conspicuous place, and sure enough, it worked. The attacker dialed in, found the documents, and spent several hours viewing and downloading them. Keeping the attacker occupied allowed Cliff to work with the German phone technicians to trace the source of the call and get one step closer to solving his mystery.

There's another interesting facet to this story. Within the cache of fake documents, Cliff included an information request template. The form mentioned a series of offline documents that authorized parties could request by mail. It contained a false name along with an address that went to LBL. It was a longshot, but Cliff was curious if the attacker would actually print, fill out, and send in the form. Sure enough, the letter showed up one day, having been sent by someone in Pittsburgh. Cliff treated the letter as evidence and sent it to the FBI, who had been working on the case with him. It would serve an essential role in characterizing the scope of the breach later on.

Did Cliff end up catching the wily hacker? You'll have to read the book he wrote about his adventure, *The Cuckoo's Egg*, to find out[1]. Regardless, Cliff Stoll gave us one of the first practical use cases for honeypots.

---

[1] Stoll, C. (1989). *The Cuckoo's Egg: Tracking a Spy Through the Maze of Computer Espionage*. Doubleday & Co.

An Evening with Berferd

In 1991, a member of the technical staff at AT&T's Bell Labs named Bill Cheswick set up a series of custom-built fake service honeypots on their outward-facing internet gateway. Partially inspired by Cliff Stoll's exploits at LBL, Cheswick was curious to see how often potential intruders attacked his network and the techniques they used. His honeypots covered a broad array of services, including FTP, Telnet, SMTP, Finger, Rlogin, and a simulated public computer system with active guest accounts.

The SMTP honeypot was particularly interesting because it allowed an attacker to exploit a notorious `SMTP DEBUG` command bug that allowed the execution of a shell script as the root user. One night, an attacker logged into the system and attempted to exploit the `SMTP DEBUG` command to send a copy of the systems `/etc/passwd` file to another compromised system they had access to at Stanford (Figure 1-1).

After some contemplation, Bill decided to send the attacker a fake passwd file and see what happened next. This decision kicked off a cat and mouse game that eventually led Bill to redirect the attacker into a carefully constructed "jailed" environment where they could execute a limited number of commands while not causing any immediate harm. Bill monitored the attacker for a while and learned about their tactics, including which vulnerabilities they might go after.

Eventually, efforts by famous names of the time like John Markoff, Tsutomu Shimomura, and Stephen Hansen led to the attacker's identification. However, he was coming from the Netherlands, where hacking wasn't illegal at the time, so no arrest was made.

Bill began referring to the attacker as Berferd because that was the username he chose to attack—an homage to *The Dick Van Dyke Show*. He would eventually write about his experience in a famous paper called *An Evening with Berferd*[2]. These adventures and the popularity of the paper helped the broader industry see the value of honeypots for luring in attackers and understanding their tools, techniques, and procedures. It also gave battle-weary defenders a framework they could imitate to "have fun" with their adversaries, which was appealing to many.

---

[2] Cheswick, B. (1992, January). "An Evening with Berferd in which a cracker is Lured, Endured, and Studied. *Proc. Winter USENIX Conference, San Francisco* pp. 20-24.

```
19:43:10 smtpd[27466]: <--- 220 inet.att.com SMTP
19:43:14 smtpd[27466]: -------> debug
19:43:14 smtpd[27466]: DEBUG attempt
19:43:14 smtpd[27466]: <--- 200 OK
19:43:25 smtpd[27466]: -------> mail from:</dev/null>
19:43:25 smtpd[27466]: <--- 503 Expecting HELO
19:43:34 smtpd[27466]: -------> helo
19:43:34 smtpd[27466]: HELO from
19:43:34 smtpd[27466]: <--- 250 inet.att.com
19:43:42 smtpd[27466]: -------> mail from: </dev/null>
19:43:42 smtpd[27466]: <--- 250 OK
19:43:59 smtpd[27466]: -------> rcpt to:</dev/^H^H^H^H^H^H^H^H^H^H^H^H^H^H^H^H^H
19:43:59 smtpd[27466]: <--- 501 Syntax error in recipient name
19:44:44 smtpd[27466]: -------> rcpt to:<|sed -e '1,/^$/'d | /bin/sh ; exit 0">
19:44:44 smtpd[27466]: shell characters: |sed -e '1,/^$/'d | /bin/sh ; exit 0"
19:44:45 smtpd[27466]: <--- 250 OK
19:44:48 smtpd[27466]: -------> data
19:44:48 smtpd[27466]: <--- 354 Start mail input; end with <CRLF>.<CRLF>
19:45:04 smtpd[27466]: <--- 250 OK
19:45:04 smtpd[27466]: /dev/null  sent 48 bytes to  upas.security
19:45:08 smtpd[27466]: -------> quit
19:45:08 smtpd[27466]: <--- 221 inet.att.com Terminating
19:45:08 smtpd[27466]: finished.
```

FIGURE 1-1:

Berferd attempting to steal the passwd file using the SMTP DEBUG command

The Honeynet Project

In 1999, an informal group of security researchers with interest in honeypot technology came together and formed a mailing list to coordinate their research activities. The group gained members as the need for expertise grew, and in 2000 they established a formal nonprofit entity called the *Honeynet Project*. The group's first board of directors included such names as Lance Spitzner, Bruce Schneier, George Kurtz, and Jennifer Granick[3].

The group viewed honeypots as serving two distinct functions: production and research. A production honeypot was one that was usually deployed inside the network and was used to detect the presence of intruders. A research honeypot was typically deployed outside the network perimeter and was used to capture attempted attacks to research new techniques and the proliferation of automated attacks.

The organization of the Honeynet Project coincided with information security entering the age of the worm. Instead of simple trojans or self-contained malware, a series of widespread vulnerabilities and poor patching practices saw an influx of malware with automated spreading capabilities. A few of the more notable instances were Code Red, NIMDA, and ILOVEYOU—all of which infected millions of hosts and made headline news. The age of the worm and a desire to concentrate attention on tracking the spread of self-propagating malware pushed the focus of the Honeynet Project firmly in the direction of research honeypots, and away from production honeypots.

---

[3] Spitzner, L. (2003). The honeynet project: Trapping the hackers. *IEEE Security & Privacy*, 99(2), 15-23.

With this focus, the Honeynet Project engaged their efforts towards the development of research honeypots in large groups called honeynets. Through four phases of development, they would go on to develop various technologies and approaches to honeynet deployment. The group gained popularity amongst the security community and eventually would support a research alliance with dozens of sub-chapters. The group was also well known for their scan of the month challenges, where they published packet capture files collected from honeypots around the world for the broader security community to analyze. I have fond memories of digging through these packets myself[4].

The timing of the group's growth, advocacy, and research combined with the age of the worm and created an interesting effect. Most information security practitioners were now aware of honeypots, but the majority only recognized their research function.

The Honeynet Project is still in existence today. Their members have produced many compelling papers, as well as two seminal books on honeypots: Lance Spitzner's *Honeypots* from 2003, and Niels Provos and Thorsten Holz's *Virtual Honeypots* from 2007. Group members support the development of various honeypot technologies, often through Google's Summer of Code program.

History Revisited

Around 2010, I began experimenting more actively with production honeypots. This work was met with resistance by those who viewed honeypots as being of research value exclusively, and I couldn't find many who were actively using honeypots to catch attackers on their network. Eventually, I was able to find a few like-minded people who believed in the value production honeypots represented.

I began writing and speaking more frequently about the topic, and eventually crystallized some of my research into a series of guidelines that organizations could use to think about and plan for the deployment of detection-oriented honeypots. Much of this research would show up in my 2013 book *Applied Network Security Monitoring*, where I dedicated an entire chapter to the idea of honeypots serving an essential role in detection infrastructure. It was here that I coined the term "Canary Honeypot" as a more descriptive name of what the Honeynet Project called production honeypots. I've since replaced Canary Honeypot with "Intrusion Detection Honeypot" to better align with IDS terminology and differentiate the word from a honeypot technology startup that uses the name Canary.

I have no way of knowing how much influence my research and book chapter had on the adoption of intrusion detection honeypots, but in 2014, I began noticing an uptick in other research in this area. When the security market began expanding rapidly, several

---

[4] You can still access these challenges at https://www.honeynet.org/challenges/.

honeypot startups (often calling themselves deception technology) emerged. The honeypot of Cliff Stoll's day was back.

Counterintelligence and Other Untold Stories

While writing this book, I spoke to many people about how they deployed honeypots in their organization. Since honeypot deployments rely on deception, it might come as no surprise that most of the people I talked to asked for me not to identify them or their companies if I discussed facets of their strategy. I believe the inherent deception honeypots rely on has also hampered their adoption, simply because there aren't as many public stories about how people use them successfully on their networks, particularly for detection purposes. Alas, my research suggests that some, particularly those who excel at secrecy, have continually used detection honeypots for quite some time.

If you look closely, you'll find things to suggest that honeypots in various forms play a role in counterintelligence operations that governments use to defend their data against competing interests. Towards the end of Cliff Stoll's Cuckoo's Egg adventure, he briefed the US National Security Agency on his techniques. He also collaborated with other investigative and intelligence services along the way with the hope that they would provide some assistance. It's reasonable to think that his unique tactics were as attractive to those organizations as his current investigation and that they might adopt some of them as well if they weren't already doing so.

Today, military officials are occasionally more open about their tradecraft as it relates to honeypots. Perusing the contract solicitations of various US government entities frequently reveals requests for bids from deception technology vendors. Uncle Sam isn't the only global player invested in honeypot technology either. In 2018, retired major general and National Security Advisor of Israel Yaakov Amidror said:

> *"There is one difference in cyber: if you are smart you do not destroy the enemy; you isolate him and give him the impression he is still active. This is a honeytrap that can be used at the right time: bring him to a place in which he can be manipulated to feel that he is still active.[5]"*

The secrecy surrounding honeypot operations ensures we'll likely never hear the specific success stories of how practitioners used honeypot technology in some environments. But like many other facets of cyber security, the ideas that spawned them eventually matriculate out into the public domain.

---

[5] Translated from Telecom News at http://bit.ly/372SyMC.

An Expanding Toolbox

As honeypot popularity grew, so too did the tools available for implementing the technology in its various forms. Let's discuss a few of the significant early contributors.

Deception Toolkit

The earliest honeypots were entirely custom for their environment, but in 1997 that changed with the release of Fred Cohen's Deception Toolkit (DTK). DTK could be installed on a system and configured to make the system appear as though it was vulnerable to one or more attacks. An attacker then probes the system, discovers the vulnerabilities, and attempts to attack it. DTK doesn't allow the attack to succeed, but it logs the attempt along with the source and payload of the attack (Figure 1-2). A savvy defender could use this information to block the attack source or build detection signatures from the payload information.

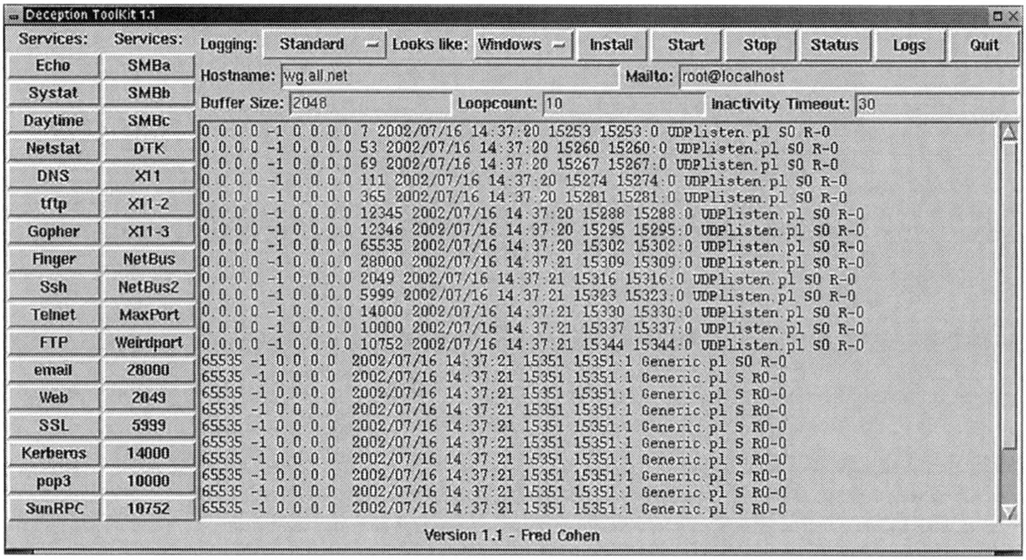

FIGURE 1-2:

The DTK Interface, an eventual part of Fred Cohen's commercial offering

Fred Cohen believed that DTK had the opportunity to make the internet much safer, collectively. It's here that he referred to honeypots as deception and introduced this technology as a method of exhausting the attacker's resources in a sort of reverse denial of service:

> *It sours the milk - so to speak. If one person uses DTK, they can see attacks coming well ahead of time. If a few others start using it, we will probably exhaust the attackers and they will go*

somewhere else to run their attacks. If a lot of people use DTK, the attackers will find that they need to spend 100 times the effort to break into systems and that they have a high risk of detection well before their attempts succeed.

If enough people adopt DTK and work together to keep it's [sic] deceptions up to date, we will eliminate all but the most sophisticated attackers, and all the copy-cat attacks will be detected soon after they are released to the wide hacking community. This will not only sour the milk, it will also up the ante for would-be copycat attackers and, as a side effect, reduce the "noise" level of attacks to allow us to more clearly see the more serious attackers and track them down[6].

While DTK wouldn't save the internet, it was a first in its class tool that inspired more development of honeypot technology.

CyberCop Sting

As free and open source honeypot tools began to see more use, it was only a matter of time before commercial honeypot offerings would become available for those looking for a turnkey solution with enterprise support. CyberCop Sting from Network Associates was released in 1999 and was one of the first products available in this space[7].

CyberCop Sting ran on a Windows NT server and could simulate an entire network segment, including routers and hosts running various platforms and services (Figure 1-3).

---

[6] *Papers about Deception* (n.d.). Retrieved December 1, 2018, from http://www.all.net/dtk/dtk.html

[7] Staff, S. V. (1999, July 14). *Network Associates Ships CyberCop Sting*. Retrieved January 22, 2019, from https://www.serverwatch.com/news/article.php/1399041/Network-Associates-Ships-Cyber-Cop-Sting.htm

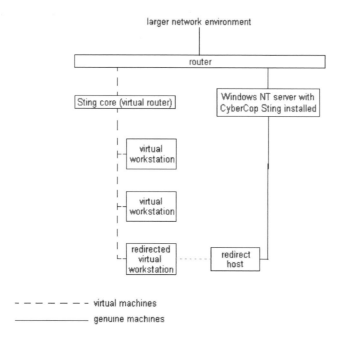

FIGURE 1-3:

CyberCop Sting as it appears on a network

The software's documentation[8] provided recommendations for internal and external deployment of the honeypot network, but most chose the external route. This was a time when people still hadn't accepted that prevention eventually fails and many felt that if they were only catching the attacker after breaking into their network, they'd already lost. But of course, we know that isn't true.

Honeyd

Neil Provos released Honeyd in 2003 as a free and open-source honeypot Swiss Army knife[9]. It was a self-contained package that ran on Windows and Unix-based systems that was easy to use and incredibly flexible, which helped it gain a wide adoption amongst information security professionals and hobbyists alike.

The honeyd binary executed with a configuration file that defined how it operates. Within the configuration file, you would define a series of networks, hosts, and services

---

[8] *CyberCop Sting guide*, Retrieved January 22, 2019, from http://www.scn.rain.com/~neighorn/PDF/Cstguide.pdf

[9] Provos, N. (2008, July 16). *Developments of the honeyd virtual honeypot*. Retrieved February 3, 2019, from http://www.honeyd.org/

that would run from a single executable (Figure 1-4). Honeyd also provided an extensive logging configuration, making it entirely self-contained without the need to rely on additional logging mechanisms. Because the tool's footprint was so small, it became elementary for users to build large honeynets containing dozens of physical hosts running thousands of fake systems and services powered by Honeyd.

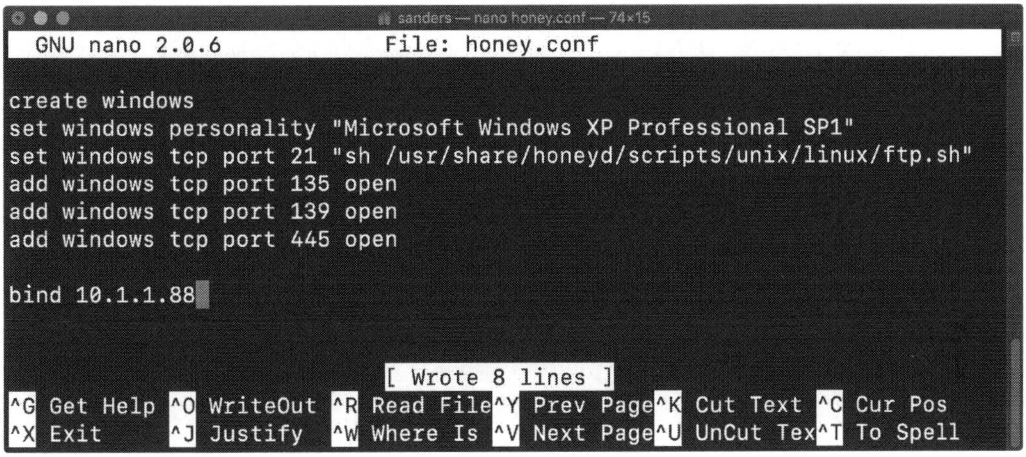

```
GNU nano 2.0.6              File: honey.conf

create windows
set windows personality "Microsoft Windows XP Professional SP1"
set windows tcp port 21 "sh /usr/share/honeyd/scripts/unix/linux/ftp.sh"
add windows tcp port 135 open
add windows tcp port 139 open
add windows tcp port 445 open

bind 10.1.1.88

                        [ Wrote 8 lines ]
^G Get Help  ^O WriteOut  ^R Read File ^Y Prev Page ^K Cut Text  ^C Cur Pos
^X Exit      ^J Justify   ^W Where Is  ^V Next Page ^U UnCut Tex ^T To Spell
```

FIGURE 1-4:

A simple Honeyd configuration file

One particularly useful feature of Honeyd was its ability to mirror specific operating system versions, as seen in the personality setting above. These profiles were based on how the popular port scanning tool nmap interprets responses from particular hosts. This feature helped make Honeyd honeypots look more convincing from the attacker's vantage point.

Honeyd was one of the most popular honeypot tools in existence. It was so flexible that it allowed users to deploy honeypots within minutes, bringing theoretical honeypots into immediate reality. Honeyd also spawned an ecosystem of related tools to help manage large deployments or visualize and analyze its output.

Modern Honeypot Tools

Around 2014, information security saw an unprecedented boom in demand and funding. This demand was met with an onslaught of new vendors and technologies that attempted to innovate with new ideas and revisit old concepts to make them useful for network defense with a modern adaptation. Honeypot technology benefited from this growth, and several deception technology-based startups have emerged since then.

A few of these include:

- **Thinkst Canary:** Founded by Haroon Meer, Canary offers low-cost software and hardware honeypots (canaries) that you can plug into a network and configure from a centralized console.
- **Cymmetria:** The MazeRunner product intercepts attackers at various points in the attack life cycle and directs them to a controlled location where their actions can be analyzed.
- **TrapX:** This solution provides a range of honeypot formats paired with visualization and analysis tools.

Along with these commercial tools, honeypots remain a point of interest for developers of free and open source software. As of this writing, I count over 80 different free honeypot tools focused across a broad spectrum of systems and services. A few examples include:

- **Cowrie**: An SSH honeypot that simulates an actual file system
- **Conpot**: An industrial control system (ICS) honeypot
- **Dionaea**: A honeypot designed to capture malware samples
- **RDPy**: A remote desktop protocol (RDP) honeypot
- **Open Canary**: A multi-service honeypot supported by Thinkst, the makers of Canary
- **Glastopf**: A web application honeypot
- **HoneyPress**: A honeypot designed to simulate the WordPress content management system

I have little doubt that we will continue to see more development of both free and commercial honeypot tools as people begin to realize the value of honeypots for low-cost, effective detection.

Conclusion

While honeypots have existed for nearly as long as information security has, using them for defense fell out of favor for some time as most focused on their research value. Information security has started to see a shift back to production honeypot usage in recent years, which sets the stage for this book. In this chapter, I traced the history of honeypots through the current period to illustrate these transitions and explain one view of why they occurred. Now, we'll leave the past behind as we define intrusion detection honeypots and how you can use them for production value as detection and network security monitoring tools.

DEFINING AND CLASSIFYING HONEYPOTS

THE HISTORY OF HONEYPOTS FROM CLIFF STOLL through the Honeynet Project and into the current era saw deception technology serve many purposes. In this chapter, I'll put some structure around honeypots by defining them, breaking them down into their common characteristics, and discussing their various goals. I'll also describe a framework for deception and where honeypots fit into this landscape. Finally, I'll explain some common criticisms of honeypots and why they're flawed.

Defining Honeypots

In 2003, Lance Spitzner published *Honeypots: Tracking Hackers*[1], one of the first books describing honeypot use in detail and one of only a few written about honeypots before this book. In his book, he said a *honeypot* is "a security resource whose value lies in being probed, attacked, or compromised." We'll adopt the same definition here.

A honeypot provides no value relevant to the core function of a business. It doesn't store customer information, process transactions, or manage logistics. It doesn't contain, process, or interpret any legitimate data used by an organization or its customers. In most

---

[1] Spitzner, L. (2003). *Honeypots: Tracking Hackers*. Reading: Addison-Wesley.

cases, a honeypot sits dormant, doing nothing until someone communicates with it. Any attempt to communicate with a honeypot is unusual because no legitimate users or applications utilize the resources provided by it.

Defining honeypots as a security resource is intentionally broad because honeypots can take many forms. The three primary types of honeypots are honey systems, services, and tokens (Figure 2-1).

A *honey system* mimics the interaction of an operating system and the services it provides. Examples include a Windows 10 system configured to act as a honeypot, or software designed to mimic the network response of a Red Hat Linux server. Anything interacting with these systems is anomalous because the honey system doesn't serve a real business purpose.

A *honey service* mimics the interaction of a specific software or protocol function. Examples include an FTP server configured with open guest access or software configured to mimic the authentication process of an SSH server. You can use a collection of several honey services to simulate an entire system. Anything interacting with these services is anomalous.

A *honey token* mimics legitimate data. Examples include a specially crafted document sitting in a protected file share, an unused user account and password, or a unique table in a SQL database. Anything that accesses, modifies, or downloads this data is abnormal.

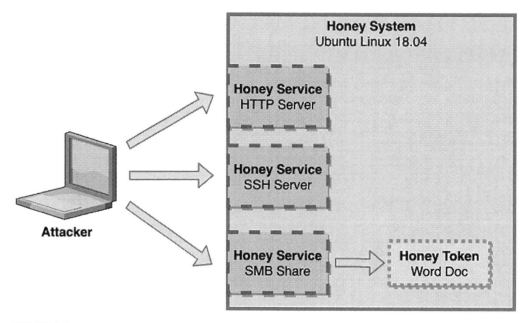

FIGURE 2-1:

Honeypots can be honey systems, services, or tokens.

While three distinct honeypot types exist, you can use them in conjunction with each other. For example, a honey system can also leverage several honey services or store honey tokens. While all three types are defined by what they attempt to mimic, their purpose is based on a few more characteristics that we'll discuss next.

Honeypot Characteristics

All honeypots are *deceptive, discoverable, interactive,* and *monitored.* But, each of these features can take many forms that ultimately define the purpose of the honeypot. I'll introduce each of these characteristics now and identify the key questions you should ask to distinguish honeypots you'll encounter and shape your honeypot deployments.

Deceptive

Deception is an advantageous distortion of perceived reality[2]. All honeypots present some form of deception by representing a false truth. While they may appear to be real systems, services, or data, they don't serve a functional purpose for a business or organization.

Barton Whaley developed one of the more widely used deception frameworks in 1982 based on a large number of use cases that included military tactics, athletes, criminals, and even magicians[3]. Whaley stated that deception is typically composed of two possible parts: hiding the real and showing the false. There are three forms of each element (Figure 2-2).

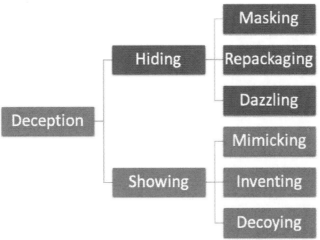

FIGURE 2-2:

Whaley's Deception Taxonomy

[2] Bell, J. B. (2017). *Cheating and deception.* Routledge.

[3] Whaley, B. (1982). Toward a general theory of deception. *The Journal of Strategic Studies,* 5(1), 178-192.

Hiding

The three forms of hiding are masking, repackaging, and dazzling. These represent level one deception because they are fundamental techniques that can stand on their own. While honeypots are never hidden entirely, you'll often hide specific features of them. Particularly, that they only serve a detection purpose.

Masking occurs when the reality is hidden by blending in with the background. The goal is invisibility, or for the deceived not to know something is there. The highest form of masking occurs when one object remains undetected amongst other nearly identical objects. For example, if I were to place a penny with the year 3020 amongst a hundred other pennies, then it's likely that my unique penny would go undetected. Another form of masking is the needle in the haystack approach. A needle is significantly different from pieces of hay, but the relative size of the needle amongst the volume of hay makes finding the needle a nearly impossible task.

Repackaging occurs when reality is hidden by a new wrapping. This form is different from masking because the goal isn't invisibility, as the deceived will know something is there without knowing its true nature. The deceived perceives the reality differently, perhaps as harmless or irrelevant. The American Civil War gives us an example of repackaging conducted by Confederate General Thomas "Stonewall" Jackson during his valley campaign in 1862. Jackson's army only had 16,000 soldiers, but he was able to force a full retreat of the Union army that was 50,000 strong. He did this by convincing the Union generals that his army was much larger than it was. During the campaign, Jackson planted spies in Union camps to spread rumors about unit sizes and movements. Throughout several battles, he strategically moved his army over vast geographic distances to engage at multiple points. As his troops forced one opposing unit to retreat, they would pull back, march a great distance, and fight another. Because each engagement appeared as though it might be different soldiers, the Union believed that Jackson's army was over 100,000 strong at one point. Eventually, Union commander Abraham Lincoln ordered a full retreat without knowing his forces dramatically outnumbered the Confederate force[4].

Dazzling occurs when the qualities of a known object are changed in such a way as to confound someone. This strategy is typically used as a last resort when masking and repackaging aren't an option, or as a backup when they fail. Encryption and obfuscation are both forms of dazzling. In this case, information is clearly there, but it may not be

---

[4] *Overview of the 1862 Stonewall Jackson Valley Campaign.* (2015, February 26). Retrieved May 1, 2018, from https://www.nps.gov/cebe/learn/historyculture/overview-of-the-1862-stonewall-jackson-valley-campaign.htm

readable without a secret key or the ability to figure out the appropriate deobfuscation technique. The complexity level of encryption or obfuscation, in theory, increases with the value of the protected data.

Showing

The three forms of showing are mimicking, inventing, and decoying. These represent level two deception, primarily because all showing involves hiding, whereas hiding almost never involves showing. Honeypots must show something for attackers to find and interact with them, so you'll use these strategies to ensure that what you're showing lures them in.

Mimicking involves selecting characteristics of another reality to create a replica of it. One of my chores as a kid was feeding the rabbits we kept in a barn next to the creek. One night, I came upon a dead possum in the rear corner of the barn, so I went to throw its carcass into the creek[5]. However, there was one major problem. As I leaned down to pick up the possum, it sprung back to life and let out a hiss that sent chills down my spine. I couldn't tell you what became of that possum because I very quickly found myself a few hundred feet away, choosing to abdicate that chore to my dad for a few days until I got up enough nerve to go back. Possums use this playing dead technique to avoid predators, as many won't eat prey that's already dead for fear of disease. The possum masked the reality that it was alive and then mimicked death. Playing dead is a survival technique found in many species in nature, and even humans will resort to it in the right circumstances.

Inventing involves the creation of a completely alternate reality rather than mimicking an existing one. The most famous example of this deception is the Trojan horse. The Greek army knew that the only way to defeat Troy was to get inside its walls, which were nearly impenetrable from the outside. Instead of a direct assault, they built a large wooden horse designed to hide a small attack force and hid the remainder of their army out of sight—a repackaging. With the actual reality hidden, this deception created the false reality that the Greeks had given up and left the horse as a peace offering while their ships were sailing for home. The Trojans took the horse inside their gates and spent hours celebrating their victory. When night fell, the repackaged soldiers departed the statue and attacked the unsuspecting city. During the chaos, they opened the gates and allowed the remaining hidden Greek forces into the city, revealing their deception. Troy had lost the battle.

Decoying involves using distraction, enticement, or a deterrent to misdirect someone away from something else. The game of football is rife with decoys. On a typical play,

---

[5] The Kentucky version of the circle of life.

the quarterback receives the ball from the snap and has a plan to throw it to a single receiver, but there may be as many as five receivers available. The receiver's goal isn't just to catch the ball. It's also to run specific routes designed to lure the defenders away from other receivers or parts of the field to create catching and maneuvering space for the intended receiver. The quarterback can also choose to stare down a specific receiver and then change his gaze to the actual intended receiver immediately before throwing (look left – pass right). If that wasn't enough, the quarterback can also pump fake his arm and pretend to throw in a particular direction without actually releasing the ball, pretend to hand the ball to a running back while still retaining possession of it, or even pretend to take off running with the ball himself before stopping quickly and heaving a long pass. A great quarterback is a master of misdirection.

Deception Taxonomy

The goal of understanding Whaley's deception taxonomy isn't to precisely classify every honeypot you create. Instead, you'll use this as a theoretical framework for the generation of honeypot ideas, ultimately building a mindset for strategic deception. Table 2-1 summarizes the different forms of hiding and showing. Because you can combine these techniques, Whaley's taxonomy represents nine potential categories of deception. For example, a honeypot could utilize masking in combination with mimicking, inventing, or decoying.

Hiding / Dissimulation	Showing / Simulation
Masking	Mimicking
Repackaging	Inventing
Dazzling	Decoying

TABLE 2-1:

Whaley's Taxonomy of Deception

All deception supports a strategic goal, whether overt and deliberate or passive and subconscious. There are countless examples of these deception techniques in nature, mostly serving to help animals find food or preventing them from becoming food. Of course, no animal has mastered deception quite like humans. We tell benign lies to protect the feelings of our friend who burnt the dinner they made for us, we exaggerate the capabilities of products we're responsible for selling, and we purposefully emit specific emotions (like sadness) to elicit a particular response from our relationship partners (like comforting). We also use these strategies to conduct war and to attack or defend information. Deception is a tool for meeting primary and secondary needs: physiological, safety, love/belonging, esteem, and self-actualization. Honeypots are merely another form of deception conjured to achieve some goal relating to these needs.

For our purposes, the type of deception will vary, based on the type of honeypot. For example, a Word document honey token placed in a folder containing several legitimate documents uses masking to appear equally as interesting but similar to the other files in the eyes of an attacker browsing the file store. A fake FTP server placed at a random location on the network uses repackaging to hide the fact that it is a honeypot, while also using mimicry to appear as though it is a legitimate application server. The combination of repackaging and mimicry is the most frequent use of deception employed by honeypots.

Keep in mind that no strategic goal is limited to a single approach or form of deception. A duck hunter will use camouflage to hide his presence, a duck call to mimic the sound of a real duck, and carved wooden ducks as decoys. Similarly, a single honeypot may employ a variety of deception strategies across an enterprise. Just like the hunter, the football quarterback, and the general, effectively accomplishing a goal benefits from diversity in deception techniques.

Discoverable

While nobody should legitimately and intentionally interact with a honeypot, you must position them so that they are discoverable and accessible within the right context. In fact, it is often the placement of the honeypot that defines its purpose. In the previous chapter, I described how Cliff Stoll gave us a lesson in discoverability when he created the fake SDINET documents, designed to keep the attacker connected to his network long enough for an engineer to conduct a trace.

He outlines his thought process in his book:

By setting our SDI files to be readable only by their owner, I made sure that nobody else would find them. Since I was the owner and the system manager, nobody else could see them. Except, perhaps, a hacker masquerading as system manager. For the hacker could still break in and become system manager. It would take him a couple of minutes to hatch his cuckoo's egg, but he'd then be able to read all the files on my system. Including those bogus SDI files. If he touched those files, I'd know about it. My monitors saved his every move. Just to make certain, though, I attached an alarm to those SDI network files. If anyone looked at them -- or just caused the computer to try and look at them -- I'd find out about it. Right away[6].

---

[6] Stoll, C. (2005). *The Cuckoo's Egg: Tracking a Spy Through the Maze of Computer Espionage*. Simon and Schuster. Page 260.

The SDINET documents, which we now call honey tokens, are only valuable to Cliff if they are in a place where an attacker is likely to discover them. On the flip side, if they are discoverable by anyone and everyone, then that may diminish the quality of the alerting achieved when legitimate users stumble upon and open the documents.

The discoverability of a honeypot requires considerations similar to the discovery of any other network asset. It's just that instead of considering what type of legitimate users need to find and access the resource, you're trying to anticipate the techniques an attacker might use or where they might end up in your network based on your threat model. In many cases, you'll place honeypots in locations where attackers are likely to discover them. When an attacker isn't likely to run across a honeypot on their own, you can leave breadcrumbs to lure them in the right direction. A *breadcrumb* is data placed on systems to intentionally lure an attacker to a honeypot. For example, leaving the URL to an HTTP honeypot in a file on a public network share. Ultimately, a honeypot should be discoverable by an attacker in one form or another.

Discoverability is primarily concerned with the placement of the honeypot: where it is relative to the edge firewall (outside/inside), what VLAN or subnet is it in, what data it's collocated with, or what sensitive assets it's near. You'll most commonly place research honeypots used to track the proliferation of worms outside the network because it should be discoverable from the public internet. That happens easiest and with the least risk when upstream from the edge firewall. This strategy contrasts sharply with a Remote Desktop Protocol (RDP) honeypot whose purpose is detecting the presence of an intruder on a specific branch of an office network. The RDP honeypot placement lies inside the network in IP space contiguous with legitimate Windows hosts that might also be running RDP.

Interactive

The success of an attacker's mission is contingent on their ability to probe their surroundings and iteratively increase their level of access in pursuit of a goal. Attackers rely on the discoverability of devices, services, and data to make this happen, which we've just discussed. Once they've discovered network assets, attackers attempt to interact with them by generating a stimulus that elicits a response. A good attacker understands the normal stimulus and response of conventional systems and services and tries to capitalize on the opportunities presented by specific or unexpected responses to stimuli they issue. For example, skilled attackers recognize the potential for SQL injection on a web server based on the responses to particular inputs.

While a honeypot may not be a real version of what it represents, it should at least appear that way to an attacker. If a system responds to a port scan and says that port 80 is open, then it should probably respond to an HTTP GET request. If an Excel spreadsheet is serving the purpose of a honey token, then a standard version of Excel should open it without error. A honeypot must be interactive and emit some response to an attacker's stimulus to get the most value from the deployment.

We categorize honeypot interactivity based on the amount and complexity of the stimulus it will respond to along a spectrum ranging from low to high interaction.

A *high interaction honeypot* is typically an entire operating system explicitly deployed to be a honeypot. It provides interaction in all the same ways that an operating system would because it often *is* just a uniquely configured OS. The high interaction level means a more significant potential to capture details about the attacker's tradecraft. The system is ideally locked down in such a way that an attacker can't compromise it and then use it to launch more attacks against the network. High interaction honeypots are what scare many away from using honeypots all together because of the overhead they represent and their potential for unexpected abuse.

Low interaction honeypots are used most often for detection. Defenders deploy them using software or scripts specifically designed to mimic one or more systems, services, or tokens. They only allow for response to a limited number of stimuli, which limits the depth of insight you can gain about the attacker. The smaller scope also shrinks the attack surface that an adversary has to work with, while still offering enough interaction to achieve the goal of the honeypot.

In most cases, a high interaction honeypot is a complete operating system deployment, and anything else is a low interaction honeypot. Some tools like the Cowrie SSH honeypot describe themselves as medium interaction because they claim to provide a much broader array of responses than a low interaction honeypot while still not allowing high interaction. The critical thing to comprehend is that interactivity exists on a continuum from low to high, rather than as two specific set points.

It's essential to consider the tradeoff between the level of interaction a given honeypot provides, the level of intelligence you can receive from it, and the effort to maintain and secure it (Figure 2-3). In general, higher interaction honeypots provide the opportunity for more intelligence, particularly when the honeypot moves beyond an individual stimulus-response. However, the intelligence return diminishes at a point in which the attacker is unlikely to take advantage of all the interactivity you're able to provide.

At the same time, the effort required to maintain and secure honeypots increases as interactivity increases. This effort grows on an exponential scale rather than a linear one as it's much more work to maintain entire operating systems than focused applications.

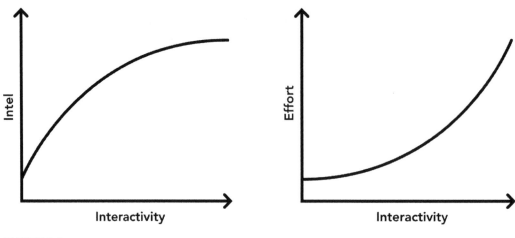

FIGURE 2-3:

The relationship between interactivity, intelligence value, and effort.

Given the risk inherent to high interaction honeypots versus how easy it is to simulate normal stimulus and response to an acceptable level, we'll focus exclusively on low-to-medium interaction honeypots in this book. In nearly every case, they provide all the functionality you'll need with significantly less work and risk.

Monitored

The final piece of the puzzle is the component that connects the actions of the attacker who discovered and interacted with the honeypot to the individual responsible for defending the network—that's you.

The basis for honeypot monitoring is simple: nobody should ever intentionally interact with a honeypot. That doesn't necessarily mean any interaction with a honeypot is malicious. It could just be that a vulnerability scanner accidentally scanned the wrong IP range, or a user got a little click-happy when browsing a file server. Nonetheless, those are still notable events and something I'd want to be aware of. A honeypot audits any interaction it experiences.

The beauty of this arrangement is that the number of false positive alerts you'll receive should be incredibly low. In most cases, it will be much lower than a traditional signature or anomaly-based intrusion detection systems, even when well-tuned. Because of this minuscule false positive rate, a properly placed honeypot is an ideal mechanism for generating alerts when interactions occur. By feeding these alerts into a SIEM or some other alerting console, the honeypot provides valuable input to your investigation pipeline.

While it may not be possible to log every command issued on every server on your network, it is possible on a honeypot because the volume should be low (or non-existent).

With most forms of logging, there are performance and analysis trade-offs, but that isn't the case with honeypots. Therefore, you should pair most honeypots with robust logging, sending events to some form of centralized log management system for use with investigations stemming from alerts.

Summarizing Honeypot Characteristics

I want you to think of the four characteristics of honeypots as categories of ingredients: fruits, vegetables, meats, and grains[7]. You must address every group to build a balanced meal, but the specific ingredients you choose and how to prepare them depends on what suits your current appetite. Similarly, the way you use deception, discoverability, interactivity, and monitoring within your honeypots depends on the strategic goals they meet. We turn to that next.

Honeypot Goals

A honeypot's value lies in being probed or attacked, but all that probing and attacking should serve a specific purpose within the context of your broader security architecture. While I described honeypots based on four main criteria, there is flexibility in how you approach each one. For example, all honeypots have to be interactive, but they can be high or low interaction. Many honeypots also mimic something else, but the subject of that mimicry goes as far as your imagination lets it. You've got room to be creative.

You can use honeypots for intrusion detection, technique and proliferation research, and resource exhaustion. Let's look at each category's typical characteristics and configuration.

Intrusion Detection

As a Kentucky kid, I grew up around coal and some folks who earned their living in the mines. If you've ever talked to miners, you know that when you start digging deep into the Earth, you're likely to encounter some unfriendly gasses that include poisonous methane. The trouble with methane is that it doesn't have a detectable odor. By the time you know you've been inhaling it, it's often too late. Before modern electronic air sensors, this problem plagued mines all over the world resulting in a large number of fatalities.

The miners eventually banded together and figured out a relatively simple solution to their problem in the form of a small yellow bird. Although the exact story is unknown, groups of miners eventually figured out that birds were much more susceptible to methane poisoning and would show effects of it well before humans. They chose canaries

---

[7] Or if you grew up in Kentucky like me, BBQ, bologna, cornbread, and Mountain Dew.

because their bright yellow color contrasted against the dark rock and took them down into the mines in cages. Everyone would keep a watchful eye on the canary. If it started acting erratically or suddenly dropped dead, the miners knew there was a problem and would evacuate the mine shaft until they could devise a plan to vent the gas. The little yellow birds saved countless lives.

The concept of the canary in the mineshaft describes the premise of intrusion detection honeypots very well. The canary is inherently more vulnerable and closely observed than the humans working around it. Similarly, an IDH is a system, service, or data . . . but one that is more vulnerable or closely observed than others.

Detection honeypots address the honeypot characteristics I described earlier in the following ways:

- **DECEPTION**: A detection honeypot usually hides its real purpose by repackaging itself as a legitimate entity. It presents itself to an attacker by mimicking a system, service, or data that already exists in your environment.

- **DISCOVERABILITY**: They're most often placed inside the network and close to the assets they mimic, usually in the same network segment, IP space, or even on the same server in the case of tokens.

- **INTERACTIVITY**: They're often low-to-medium interaction since any interaction at all constitutes an alert-worthy event.

- **MONITORING**: Interaction logging is robust. Most initial interactions generate alerts fed into an alert console, SIEM, or third-party managed security service provider.

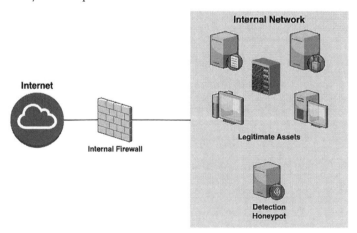

FIGURE 2-4:

Typical Detection Honeypot Deployment

In theory, if an attacker compromises the network, they will attempt to interact with the honeypot too at some point. For example, if an attacker gains access to a range of database servers and a honeypot is among them, they'll eventually interact with the honeypot along with the legitimate servers. While it isn't feasible to alert on every access to a legitimate production server due to the volume of connections, alerting on any interaction with a honeypot is perfectly manageable. There shouldn't be anything else happening there.

Detection honeypots come in many forms and are ripe for creative approaches. Some common examples include:

A honey system mimicking a Cisco router. This honeypot is discoverable from inside the network and presents a login prompt when someone connects to it over telnet or SSH. It may let an attacker authenticate and issue commands to provide more data to help the defender ascertain the attacker's goal. Any connection to this system generates an alert, and it logs all login attempts and commands.

A honey service mimicking an industrial control system (ICS) human-machine interface console. This honeypot is discoverable from inside the network on a segment containing other ICS assets. It has the same interface as other HMIs, perhaps via Telnet/SSH or HTTP. Interaction with the on-screen commands provides some feedback to indicate something meaningful occurred without actually connecting to production equipment. Any connection to the system generates an alert and logs all commands and interactions.

A honey token in the form of a dormant user account in Microsoft Active Directory. The account is based on a fake person who exists in application and personnel databases as though they were real. Strategically placed documents that attackers are likely to find list the username as a privileged user. At some point, an attacker finds a reference to this account and attempts to log in to a system with the username. However, the account is disabled or restricted from authenticating to any systems. Windows logs any login attempts using the account or attempts to manipulate the account itself. Any activity related to this account represents abnormal activity, so the Windows logs generate alerts fed into an IDS console or SIEM.

Because detection honeypots are the primary focus in this book, we'll take a more in-depth look at each of these strategies in later chapters.

Technique and Proliferation Research

The most common way to learn about something that you don't understand is to observe it, and nobody knows that better than disease researchers. When scientists discover a new virus, they take great care to obtain a sample and set up a test environment. They populate that test environment with a variety of human cells from different parts of the body to facilitate a set of experiments. In each trial, they carefully release the virus in a controlled manner, exposing it to arrays of cells. Then, they watch. They're concerned with how the virus interacts with the cells if it does at all, how specific cells attempt to fight off the infection, and how the virus might evolve over multiple exposures.

The careful observation of the living virus is what helps epidemiologists characterize diseases, develop vaccinations and cures for them, and ultimately contain outbreaks. And, it's all based on controlling a finite number of variables, waiting, and watching. This level of observation is the same technique used by biologists to study animals, by psychologists to study people, and by information security practitioners to study attackers.

Technique and proliferation honeypots have the following characteristics:

- **DECEPTION**: A research honeypot usually hides its real purpose by repackaging itself as a legitimate entity. It presents itself to an attacker by mimicking a system or service, but not necessarily one that exists in your network environment.

- **DISCOVERABILITY**: They're placed outside the network or in a DMZ so that attackers can easily discover them with network scanning. The goal is to lure in opportunistic attackers and entice them to pounce on a host that appears vulnerable.

- **INTERACTIVITY**: Most research honeypots are exposed to some type of attack, or at least made to look that way. For example, an out-of-date web server with multiple buffer overflow vulnerabilities would invite HTTP and web server attacks for study. These honeypots range from low to high interaction. You must give special care to ensure attackers can't pivot from compromised honeypots into the internal network.

- **MONITORING**: Interaction logging is robust, but generally not paired with alerting. Researchers review the output from recorded interactions only periodically since these attacks are against systems isolated from production networks.

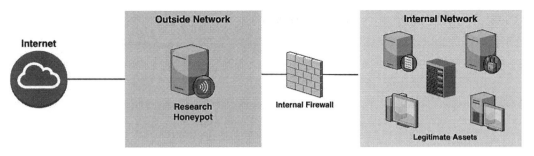

FIGURE 2-5:

Typical Research Honeypot Deployment

If a research honeypot is successful at eliciting attacks, you'll be rewarded with examples of tools and techniques used to exploit the services you've exposed. Earlier in my career, this helped me learn about how attackers probe systems for vulnerabilities, inject stimuli and monitor valuable responses, and use code obfuscation techniques to mask exploits. It also helped me better understand that a single vulnerability might be exploited in hundreds of ways, so detection based on one of those methods has limited value.

The era of the worm in the 2000s saw research honeypots demonstrate value for tracking the proliferation of self-replicating code. Like a disease, worms start from "patient zero" and spread by exploiting specific vulnerabilities. The Code Red and NIMDA worms were two of the more famous specimens of this era. The organizations that deployed externally accessible honeypots were among the first to know about these worms and dissect them to build protection and detection signatures. Larger companies, antivirus vendors, and independent researchers used networks of honeypots (honeynets) to track and assess the global impact of the malware. More recently, external-facing honeypots were used to track the proliferation of the SMB worms Wannacry and NotPetya, both based on the EternalBlue exploit and used to deliver ransomware.

When many people think of honeypots, it's these research honeypots that come to mind because of their popularity during the era of the worm (as discussed in Chapter 1). However, their value proposition is limited. First and foremost, technique and proliferation honeypots aren't useful for detecting real attacks against your network, only opportunistic ones thrown against external-facing infrastructure. Even if structured adversaries[8] conducted targeted attacks against those devices, it probably wouldn't be feasible to differentiate them from the voluminous opportunistic attacks. Simple port and vulnerability scans alone dominate the logs of externally facing honeypots.

---

[8] Structured adversaries are organized and usually have significant resources. They often attack targets for specific reasons pertaining to their strategic goals.

Since these honeypots are of no real production value, most choose to set them up as a learning exercise. As I mentioned, they can provide useful insight and data to dig through. However, this too is of less value today because there are so many other great sources of data related to opportunistic attacks and malware. More people are writing, blogging, and sharing attack technique data now than ever before, and consuming that information is usually more efficient for learning than setting up honeypots in this style.

Resource Exhaustion

In business, we would like to believe that the only strategy for beating your competition is having a better product and letting the cream rise to the top. However, it's not that simple. Better products and companies often lose because of, you guessed it . . . deception. Consider two pizzerias in the same small town, Atlas Pizza and Snappy Tomato. Because the number of customers in town is limited, they compete fiercely for business. On a busy Saturday night, the owner of Snappy Tomato has a brilliant idea. He disguises his voice and adorns a fake name before calling Atlas and ordering twenty pizzas with complex and unusual combinations of toppings[9]. The order creates a real hassle at Atlas because it jams up their production. So many pizzas at once tie up the hands of the cook and consume space in the ovens. A massive delay in service leaves customers unhappy, and they might just consider Snappy Tomato next time they get a pizza craving. Of course, the owner of Snappy Tomato never shows up to claim these pizzas, so this deception only cost him the time it took to make a phone call.

This scenario is an example of a resource exhaustion attack. A restaurant has a finite number of employees to make the pizza and just a few ovens to cook it. By exceeding the capacity of those resources, others who are competing for them get sent to the back of a slow-moving line. This scenario also describes honeypots used for resource exhaustion.

Resource exhaustion honeypots have the following characteristics:

- **DECEPTION**: These honeypots usually hide their true purpose by repackaging themselves as a legitimate entity. They present themselves to an attacker by mimicking a system or service that exists in your network environment. They also serve as a decoy to draw some attention away from legitimate production entities.

- **DISCOVERABILITY**: Resource exhaustion honeypots are most often placed outside the network to tie up the efforts of opportunistic attackers exploring your external-facing IP space. Inside the network, they're deployed

---

[9] For the record, I don't consider pineapple a sin against pizza. But, I'm a Ham and Pepperoni guy.

for slowing the progress of structured adversaries who've made their way through the perimeter. In either deployment, these honeypots should be numerous in quantity. You might deploy dozens or even hundreds of honeypots that mimic a single system, service, or token. I've seen a few networks with tens of thousands of honeypots serving this role, managed as a fleet.

- **INTERACTIVITY**: They are almost always low interaction since you'll deploy them in large numbers. The interaction they provide should be nearly identical to legitimate resources, but the complexity should increase to waste attacker time and effort. Special applications allow honeypot operators to artificially slow down network traffic or create labyrinths of false or recursive interaction points.

- **MONITORING**: Logging is less robust than other types of honeypots since the amount of interaction can be overwhelming, by design. When deployed inside the network and paired with the detection function, most initial interactions generate alerts fed into an alert console, SIEM, or third-party managed security service provider.

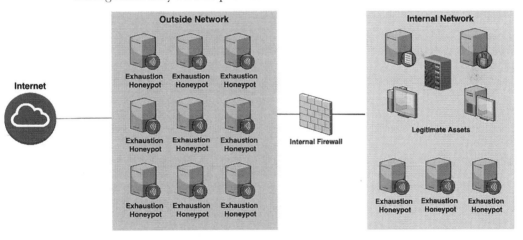

FIGURE 2-6:

Typical Resource Exhaustion Honeypot Deployment

The goal is for these honeypots to waste as much of the attacker's time as possible by deploying a large number of honeypots that allow enough interaction to appear real and keep the bad guys interested[10]. Consider a scenario where you are required to

---

[10] LaBrea is another historical example and was one of the first deliberate resources exhaustion honeypots. Learn more about it at https://labrea.sourceforge.io/Intro-History.html.

expose a web server to the internet. An opportunistic attacker might scan the web server looking for specific directories that indicate the presence of particular vulnerabilities or unintentionally disclosed sensitive information. Here, you can deploy a tool like WebLabyrinth[11] to create a unique directory on the server. When the attacker's scanner requests this directory, WebLabyrinth creates several bogus web pages the scanner will then request. When the scanner requests those pages, WebLabyrinth creates more bogus pages. This process repeats on and on, tying up the scanner indefinitely. I've seen more than a few attackers wander into this trap, get frustrated, and leave the web server behind all together.

You can deploy resource exhaustion honeypots inside the network, but their value is limited there. In that case, any observed interaction will kick off the incident response process, so you're often less concerned about slowing the attacker down and more concerned with immediate containment and eradication. For some organizations that are concerned with threat intelligence and attribution tied to structured adversaries, slowing the attacker down and observing them may be desirable. It can also buy time for defenders to identify, contain, and eradicate the attacker before they do more damage. In these cases, resource exhaustion honeypots are an excellent fit to keep the fish on your line for a bit longer. That isn't realistic for most organizations due to the effort of maintaining a resource exhaustion honeypot fleet.

Summarizing Honeypot Goals

These three honeypot goals aren't the only uses for honeypot technology, but they are the most common and the most practical. You can combine the functionality of certain types of honeypots. For example, you can use most internal resource exhaustion honeypots as detection honeypots. Proliferation research honeypots can also contain functions that exhaust attacker resources as well. This book focuses almost exclusively on intrusion detection honeypots, which are the most valuable for network defenders.

Common Misconceptions About Honeypots

The rest of the book is devoted to teaching you ideas and strategies for making your detection honeypot deployment successful. But before we get there, I want to highlight how most honeypots fail before they're ever deployed. The problem usually centers around misconceptions about what honeypots are and what they do. I want to now address some of those things directly.

---

[11] You can download WebLabyrinth here: https://github.com/mayhemiclabs/weblabyrinth

"Honeypots are complex and expensive to maintain . . ."

This may be true of high interaction honeypots, but most intrusion detection honeypots (and indeed the ones I advocate in this book) are low interaction. You'll often deploy them using incredibly simple applications or scripts you can set up with a minimal amount of system resources. Small servers can host hundreds of honeypots since they aren't serving production data and sit dormant most of the time. Additionally, these honeypot tools integrate with existing logging and monitoring applications when anomalous interaction occurs. Above all else, detection honeypots come in a variety of forms. There are techniques that fit nearly every budget.

"Honeypots are only useful as a research tool . . ."

This is only true of technique and proliferation research honeypots, but they are only one of a few ways you can use honeypots. Lower interaction honeypots placed inside the network designed to mimic real assets are great detection tools and simple to deploy and maintain.

"I'm not ready for honeypots . . ."

I spend a lot of time talking to people about the maturity of their detection program. For most medium to large organizations, it makes sense to start with simple indicator matching and signature-based intrusion detection systems. After that, I firmly believe honeypots are the next logical step and that you should deploy them well ahead of sophisticated machine learning or statistical detection tools. Honeypots are well within the realm of feasibility for most organizations.

One of the real benefits of honeypots is that they are one of the few solutions that scale down even better than they scale up. Small businesses struggle because they often don't have any dedicated security staff. This limitation means they can't afford the management or tuning overhead that comes with IDS or SIEM. The deployment effort for one or two low interaction honeypots, along with the minimal maintenance requirement, makes them an ideal starting point for small businesses. Instead of piping their alerts to an alerting console, you can send them to an email mailbox or Slack channel. Honeypots are the most cost-effective starting place for smaller organizations. With this in mind, I advocate for honeypots as a requirement for nearly any organization. I've not yet seen a network that I didn't think could benefit from at least one type of intrusion detection honeypot.

"An attacker can easily figure out that this is a honeypot . . ."

In many cases, this is correct. But, by that point, it doesn't matter! When using honeypots for detection, any interaction at all constitutes an alert-worthy event. So, by the time the attacker discovers they're interacting with a honeypot, you are already hot on their trail. If you're able to provide more layers of deception and interaction to learn about the attacker's tradecraft, that's a positive. But it's certainly not required to achieve the primary benefit of detection honeypots.

"An attacker can compromise a honeypot and use it to pivot to real production hosts . . ."

This is a real concern with high interaction honeypots, as you're trying to give an attacker limited access to an entire operating system. The delicate balance between enough access to collect interesting data but not enough access to allow pivoting or cause damage is tricky, and requires a great deal of effort due to the attack surface. This scenario is one reason why high interaction research honeypots are usually placed outside the firewall and isolated at the network layer. Lower interaction honeypots are preferred for most internal applications as they have a dramatically lower attack surface. For an attacker to turn their access to a low interaction honeypot into a more substantial compromise, they would likely need to exploit a vulnerability in the honeypot software itself. Lower interaction means smaller attack surface and decreased opportunity for those attacks to occur. That doesn't mean that it is impossible, but for simple scripts or service-specific honeypots, it's unlikely. Nonetheless, if an attacker attempts to exploit a honeypot, then you've already been alerted to the initial interaction and should already be in the midst of the incident response process because it means the attacker is inside your network.

Conclusion

I dedicated this chapter to defining honeypots, describing their common characteristics, and identifying the different configurations of those characteristics in support of specific goals. Honeypots are rooted in the psychology of deception. So, we discussed a taxonomy of deception to characterize the nature of honeypot usage better and help you start thinking with a deception-oriented mindset. Finally, I provided an overview of some common reasons why honeypot deployments fail before they get started and why those concerns are misguided. In the next chapter, I'll lay out a framework for honeypot planning before we get to work building and deploying honeypots.

PLANNING HONEYPOT-BASED DETECTION 3

YOU SHOULD NOW HAVE A GOOD UNDERSTANDING OF the history and concept of honeypots, along with the characteristics they have in common and the purpose they serve. In this chapter, I'll explain the process of planning your very own detection honeypot deployment. I'll describe the deception planning process, how to best determine honeypot placement, and walk through a case study where I apply these concepts. In short, I'll help you figure out what honeypots to build and where to place them.

Deception Framework: See – Think – Do

A detection honeypot achieves its goal when unwanted intruders probe or access it. Achieving this goal sounds simple in theory, but making efficient and effective use of honeypot deployments requires thoughtful planning and knowledge of your network. Many honeypot deployments fail because the security practitioner doesn't think about how their goals relate to the attacker they're trying to deceive.

Successful honeypots demonstrate a defender's ability to control an attacker through deception.

You want the attacker to *SEE* systems, services, or data that are actually honeypots.

You want the attacker to *THINK* the honeypots are valuable.

You want the attacker to *DO* something that causes an interaction with the honeypot.

You win if you control these three things. When the attacker interacts with the honeypot, you'll know they're on your network and can watch them as you start an incident response (Figure 3-1).

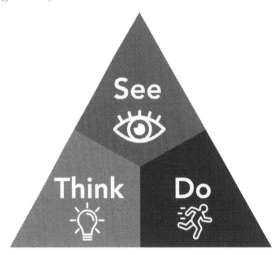

FIGURE 3-1:

Control via the See-Think-Do Deception Methodology

We'll refer to this process collectively as the See-Think-Do Deception Methodology. The US Military (in a Joint Chiefs of Staff publication) designed it to plan operational deception in support of strategic goals[1]. It isn't specific to honeypots or information security, but it provides an excellent framework for planning deception in networks.

For the attacker to DO something, they must also SEE and THINK something. Most failures getting attackers to interact with honeypots are a failure in making them visible (SEE) and making them mimic something interesting (THINK). Let's walk through each of these deception planning steps.

Honeypot Visibility (See)

I want you to imagine you're a criminal mastermind planning to steal money from a bank during the middle of the night. You'll probably focus most of your effort on gaining initial access to the building and gaining access to the vault where the money is stored. The

---

[1] https://info.publicintelligence.net/JCS-MILDEC.pdf

reasons are clear: the doors and windows are the only way into the building and the vault contains the cash you're after.

Of course, the bank knows this too. They focus most of their security controls in these locations. The doors have several industrial grade locks, thick steel mesh covers the windows, and the vault is, well . . . a vault. It's not just about protective controls, though. The bank knows that if someone successfully bypasses physical prevention, they'll still wind up at one of these ingress points or in the vault. That's why they also deploy detective controls like alarm systems or monitoring controls like cameras. You must plan for honeypot visibility using a similar mindset. The two most effective strategies for planning honeypot visibility are focusing on common footholds and valuable assets.

Common Footholds (Outside-In)

If you wish to control what your attacker sees, you have to know where they will be. Just like the doors and windows represent places a criminal is likely to enter a bank, we have similar locations in the network. *Common footholds* are network locations where an attacker is likely to enter the network and gain initial access. These are usually:

- **User Workstations**: The most straightforward way for attackers to gain access to a system is to trick a user into clicking a link, opening an email attachment, or interacting with a malicious document. Any of these things could lead to a compromise. User workstations are generally the most common location where an attacker gains their initial foothold. They're also where insiders are most likely to launch attacks from.

- **Externally Facing Infrastructure**: Anything exposed to the internet presents an attack surface that miscreants can poke around at. Eventually, they may discover a vulnerability that leads to some control over these assets. While this can be the result of unpatched application vulnerabilities, these days it's usually through web application attacks such as SQL injection. This includes externally facing infrastructure hosted on your own network and with cloud service providers.

- **VPN IP Ranges:** Attackers who have stolen legitimate credentials will often connect to a network as though they were an authorized user with VPN access. Without additional controls in place, this could place their system directly on the network as though they were permitted to be there.

An attacker who gains access in a common foothold will almost certainly pillage the device they're connected to first if it contains anything valuable. But this location doesn't just represent the first victim; it also represents the beachhead where the attacker gains a vantage point and from where they'll launch other attacks.

From there, the attacker begins the process of iterative discovery to move to other hosts. *Iterative discovery* occurs when an attacker uses a variety of techniques to learn more about the network and its assets to expand a compromise (or what some would call lateral movement). You can think of this as though the attacker is standing on top of the castle walls looking inward towards their goal, which is why this is also called the outside-in strategy.

Ask yourself, what can the attacker see from the common footholds on my network? If you successfully identify the common footholds and what iterative discovery techniques attackers can use effectively from them, you should be positioned to ensure honeypots are visible in these scenarios.

As an example, consider an attacker that has gained access to a user workstation (Figure 3-2). They pillage all of the locally stored data in the victim's profile before turning their attention to iterative discovery. They'll attempt to enumerate network shared drives and folders linked to the workstation, scan the network segment for other reachable systems, or even perform passive reconnaissance by watching for network connections to systems with a pathway to the compromised host. These discovery actions increase the visibility of the attacker and help them choose their next victim. It also defines the conditions where your honeypot must be accessible. If the attacker is searching for shared folders, you could provide one by mapping a drive to a honeypot. Similarly, if they are scanning for other systems, you can create a honeypot that responds to them.

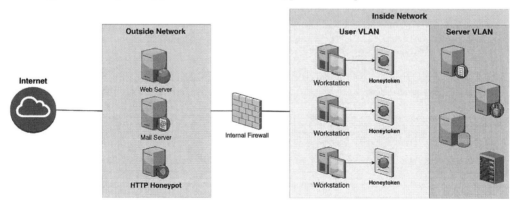

FIGURE 3-2:

The outside-in strategy focuses on honeypot placement near common footholds

Honeypot placement based on common footholds is useful for detecting both opportunistic and targeted attacks from structured or unstructured adversaries, since they'll both leverage common footholds. These honeypots are more numerous since there may be a lot of common footholds in an organization.

Valuable Assets (Inside-Out)

The bank vault represents where it holds its most valuable assets, making it the target of any would-be criminal. What are the most valuable assets on your network? Consider the following scenario to help you decide:

It's 4:30 PM on a Friday and you're just about to cut out a bit early to get a jumpstart on your weekend. As it always seems to happen, a new critical alert pops into your IDS console. Now, pause for a moment and think about that alert. What could that alert tell you that would make your stomach sink and force you to break out into a cold sweat? What could it say that immediately makes you realize your weekend plans are kaput?

The answer to this scenario is probably a good starting point. If all else fails, walk up to your boss and ask him in the creepiest voice possible, "What's your biggest fear?"

That might freak them out[2], but once you work past it you should achieve insight into the biggest threats to your organization. You'll probably have to translate those from business risk into technical risk centered around breakdowns in confidentiality, integrity, or availability of data. Your findings will be dependent on the mission of your organization. Consider these examples:

- An online retailer is concerned about the availability of its website because seconds of downtime equates to millions of dollars lost. An attack on their web or database servers could manifest in a large amount of downtime.

- A pharmaceutical research organization is concerned about the confidentiality of its drug formulas and their manufacturing process. An attack on research systems or sensitive file servers could cause their formulas to fall into the hands of a competitor or become public, resulting in a massive loss of revenue.

- A legal firm is concerned about the integrity of the communication between the firm and its clients. An attack on their file or email server that results in the modification of contracts or correspondence could result in costly legal complications and harm their reputation.

All attackers want to steal something from you. That something might be direct like money or intellectual property. It might also be indirect, like damaging your reputation or denying access to resources. In either case, the technical assets where these things exist

---

[2] On second thought, some of you probably have really creepy voices. Maybe stick with a normal voice and make it clear what your point is.

represent a convergence point where you're likely to deploy honeypots.

You will formulate this approach not from the perspective of the attacker with a new foothold looking into your network from its outskirts, but instead from your perspective at the valuable assets you're trying to protect looking outward toward your network borders. That's why it's also referred to as an inside-out strategy.

For example, consider an attacker that compromised the pharmaceutical research company mentioned above. They're specifically targeting the organization to steal data related to the development and manufacturing of the firm's drugs. Through the process of iterative discovery, they eventually figure out the information they want is on a file server on the research network. When the attacker eventually accesses the file server, your honeypot should be present. This likely includes honey files or directories collocated with legitimate sensitive data.

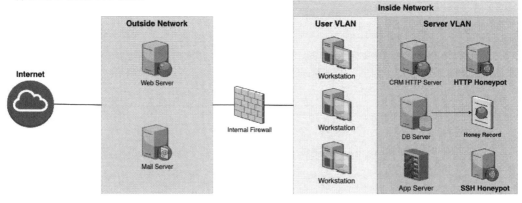

FIGURE 3-3:

The inside-out strategy focuses on honeypot placement near sensitive assets and data

Honeypot placement based on valuable assets is most useful for detecting targeted attacks because these adversaries are most likely to pursue specific data and have the resources and persistence to get there. These honeypots are less numerous since most networks consolidate valuable assets in only a few locations.

With your honeypot visible, you're in control of what the attacker sees. Now you must control what they think by building meaningful characteristics into your honeypot.

Honeypot Mimicry (Think)

Going back to the bank example, let's say that you've managed to sneak into the vault, and you're rewarded by finding a pallet full of cash. It's way more cash than you can carry, but you go ahead and try to grab as much as you can. You stuff a duffel bag so full it's about to pop, you fill your pockets, you stuff the inside of your coat, and you even tuck a few stacks under your stylish criminal hat before running back out through the exit. However, what you don't see is that when you walked through the door, you passed by a radio transmitter. The transmitter triggers a sensor located in the hollowed-out center of a stack of bills. Ten seconds later, an incendiary device ignites, makes a loud pop, and you find yourself covered with bright blood-red colored dye. You're panicked, the noise has drawn attention to you, and you're not entirely sure what's just happened. In your distress, you just drop the money and run.

This ruse is made possible because of mimicry and controlling what the criminal thinks. The fake stack of bills looked just like the regular stack without revealing the repackaging deception of the hidden dye pack. Anyone who breaches the vault attempts to steal piles of cash because they have value, are easily portable, and are exposed (unlike other valuables that might exist in individual lockboxes).

We can apply this same principle to network assets by mimicking something valuable. There are two strategies: create something uniquely interesting that stands out or blend in amongst other valuable things that already exist on your network.

Stand Out

Humans notice things that are unique or different when they're paying appropriate attention or not otherwise distracted. That's why you'll see a dead pixel on the screen of your TV or a small stain on your shirt. It's also why you're successful in investigations that are contingent on spotting things that just don't make sense, like a suspicious URL. If we combine our natural ability to detect things that are unique with the curiosity innate in humans (and especially in infosec practitioners and attackers), you have the ingredients necessary to direct and control attention.

> *NOTE: The regulation of attention and how it affects perception is a hot topic for psychology research. You may be familiar with the experiment where people watch a video while counting the number of passes made by a basketball team. During the video, a person in a gorilla costume walks right into the middle of the screen, does a little dance, and walks off. People counting passes are so focused on this task that over 50% of them don't notice the gorilla at all, despite it being directly in their field of vision[3]. You can apply lessons learned from experiments on attention to many fields, but perhaps none more so than the area dedicated exclusively to drawing attention and soliciting action—marketing. Honeypots are, in some part, an exercise in manipulating attackers' attention.*

A system, service, or data that stands out among the things around it has gravity,

---

[3] Chabris, C., & Simons, D. (2010). *The Invisible Gorilla: And Other Ways Our Intuitions Deceive Us.* Harmony.

drawing attackers toward it and increasing the odds they'll eventually interact with it. To illustrate the value of standing out, I recently created five honey services that mimicked a web server with a simple HTML webpage and a login form that appeared real but didn't actually perform authentication. The honeypots were all identical with one exception: they each had unique names in the HTML title tag of their otherwise minimal index pages. Those names were:

- Server 1
- Server 2
- Server 3
- SPACKLE
- Server 5

The word SPACKLE doesn't have any special meaning; I just think it's a fun word. I placed all five honeypots in contiguous IP space and made them accessible to the public internet. After a few weeks, I gathered data on all of the interactions with the honeypots. The SPACKLE honeypot saw twelve times more interaction than the other four, including more password guessing and SQL injection attempts. This increased interaction was all by virtue of standing out amongst a crowd. Attackers thrive on spotting unique things, so give it to them!

Consider the earlier example of the attacker that compromised the pharmaceutical company looking for specific drug manufacturing data. Eventually, they'll land on a system in the research network segment with access to the file server containing this information, either directly or through a system with remote access over the network. Since you know where the attacker will be looking, you know where your honeypot should be visible, so now you must make it look enticing.

This scenario provides a perfect opportunity to create a honey token that stands out. For example, if the top-level directory of a folder contains hundreds of Microsoft Word documents, create a PDF honey token that alerts when opened. To make it stand out more, you could give it an enticing name like "Pharma Supplier Information.pdf" or even place the name in all caps. Whatever the characteristics of the other files in the directory are, you want to do something different. You can leverage document type, file name, file size, and more.

Name	Date modified	Type	Size
may party.docx	5/4/2020 10:13 AM	Microsoft Word D...	1,812 KB
Outline specs 2.docx	5/4/2020 10:12 AM	Microsoft Word D...	39 KB
Outline specs.docx	4/15/2020 3:17 PM	Microsoft Word D...	20 KB
Q1 20 report.docx	4/15/2020 3:17 PM	Microsoft Word D...	20 KB
Q2 20 report.docx	4/14/2020 4:07 PM	Microsoft Word D...	18 KB
SUPPLIER LIST.xlsx	5/4/2020 10:12 AM	Microsoft Excel W...	4,139 KB

FIGURE 3-4:

The honey token stands out based on the unique name, file type, and capitalization

To stand out, a honeypot should mimic a system, service, or data that is remarkably different from other visible things. You want the attacker to think they are real, valuable assets. Remember, your goal is to capture the attention of the attacker so that they'll eventually interact with the honey token. A great way to do that is uniqueness. This tactic works well in many situations but excels when you surround the honeypot by a large number (at least dozens or hundreds) of similar items. I often rely on standing out in two situations: honey tokens placed amongst legitimate data, or honey systems and servers mimicking traditionally easy-to-compromise targets for attackers--things like older operating systems, web servers running content management systems (WordPress or Joomla), or remote access tools (VNC, LogMeIn).

Blend In

We often think of attention as binary; you pay attention to something or you don't. In reality, you should think of attention as something that exists on a spectrum from low to high. If you've been driving for a while, then traversing a familiar route is something that won't necessarily command a great deal of attention. That's why you feel comfortable driving to work while eating breakfast, talking on the phone, or rocking out to the newest Sturgill Simpson song[4]. Contrast this with your first time driving in a new city or trying to find a location you haven't been to before. You've probably turned the radio down and gotten off the phone so you can devote your attention to your surroundings and the directions you're attempting to follow. In both instances, you're paying attention to driving, but are leveraging very different amounts of it.

When you build honeypots that stand out, you're attempting to draw an attacker's full attention. This effort requires the creation of something remarkably different from the things around it and can be challenging. The good news is that sometimes, drawing only a part of

---

[4] I don't recommend doing all this at the same time.

an attacker's attention is good enough. Instead of creating something unique, you instead seek to blend in with something that is already interesting and likely to gain their attention.

This strategy is precisely what I described in the bank vault scenario, where the thief snatched a stack of bills containing a dye pack because it blended in with legitimate money. Blending in is a much easier strategy in this example because to stand out would require a level of extravagance that might be significant work or might generate suspicion on the part of the thief. If you walked into a bank vault and something resembling the Hope Diamond was just sitting there, you'd probably figure out that's a trap and gravitate towards the paper currency anyway.

Building honeypots that blend in with other valuable assets effectively makes an attacker believe the honeypot is also valuable. In a previous example, I described an attacker who compromised a user's workstation. One iterative discovery technique nearly all attackers use is to enumerate shared drives and folders linked to the system. These typically connect back to shared file servers that are likely to contain a treasure trove of valuable information. This situation provides the perfect opportunity to blend in by creating a file system honeypot. Once you've created a shared folder on a server, you leave a breadcrumb by mapping a drive to it from workstations. The attacker isn't just going to pick one or two network drives to browse; they're going to dig through all of them! Ideally, the drive and honeypot have names consistent with others that the attacker sees. If there is a mapped drive called "RESEARCH1 on FS1," you would create another called "RESEARCH2 on FS2." The honeypot won't provide value to the attacker, but they don't know that. Because it appears similar to the shared drive that does provide value, the honeypot is valuable by association.

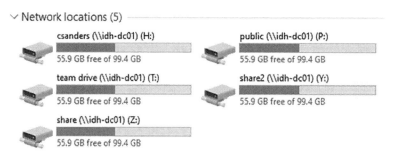

FIGURE 3-5:

Which one of these is the honeypot? You can't tell, and the attacker can't either.

A wonderful thing about detection honeypots is that blending in and standing out are both useful strategies that are likely to spur attacker interaction. Standing out is often easier because default and minimally configured honeypots inherently stand out in many ways. Building honeypots that blend in requires deliberate effort. Be conscious of the time you spend making your honeypots blend in, as you'll eventually see diminishing returns from that effort. Regardless, both strategies can be effective.

Once a honeypot is seen by an attacker, your next concern is to make them think it has value. If you're familiar with your network and where valuable information exists, then you already know what someone is looking for and where they're looking for it. So, give it to them. You now control what the attacker sees and thinks. The final step is to control what they do.

Honeypot Interactivity (Do)

The dye packs hidden amongst bank bills work because a thief interacts with them in the same way they would with the legitimate bills, by physically taking them out of the building. Similarly, you must present the level of interaction with honeypots to the attacker in a way consistent with how they would expect to interact with the asset you're mimicking.

You've ensured the attacker sees your honeypots whenever they encounter sensitive business assets, and you've mimicked those assets so that they think they are legitimate systems serving a similar function. Now, you just need them to do something—to interact with the honeypot. Your honeypot should provide enough interaction so that it is capable of triggering a notifying event. In the case of the file system honeypot I've discussed, a user merely accessing a shared folder constitutes that event. This event could also be someone attempting to log into a service, sending packets to a system, or opening a file. The event must be observable and recorded (Figure 3-6).

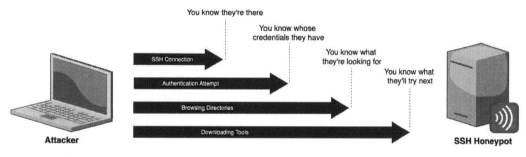

FIGURE 3-6:

When the attacker does something with the honeypot, you'll know they're there. The more they interact, the more you'll know about them.

The goal of a honeypot is to provide a notification that can lead to an alert. Still, the best honeypots also offer an additional layer of context through the interaction they provide. Consider an SSH honeypot that listens on port 22 and generates an alert when someone attempts to connect to it. That would be useful by itself, but you can go farther by implementing a honey service that simulates SSH more thoroughly, like Cowrie. Not only will you be able to alert when an attacker connects, but you can also prompt them to provide a username and password. If they've stolen legitimate credentials and attempt to use them, you'll know whose credentials they obtained. This knowledge is a significant input to the incident response process because you can immediately start to center investigation and containment around that user and things they can access. Going farther, these SSH honeypot applications can also simulate a file system. This feature gives you a window into what data the attacker looks for and the commands they attempt to run. I've used this technique several times to uncover related attacker infrastructure when they try to download additional tools to compromise systems.

You'll gain additional insight through a higher degree of interaction in honey tokens that mirror legitimate files such as MS Office documents or PDFs. The minimum interaction needed for alerting can be found simply by logging when someone opens, copies, or moves the file. You can go farther by embedding a link to a server you control within the file. If the attacker exfiltrates the file, they'll eventually open it or pass it off to someone who does. If they're not carefully monitoring their outbound connections, the file calls back to the hidden link when it's opened. This result places the IP address of the person opening the file into your logs and can aid in attribution or prosecution.

While questions of visibility and mimicry are focused on the needs of the attacker, the issue of interaction focuses on you and the information you desire to capture when someone accesses your honeypots. A minimally valuable honeypot must provide an alert when interaction occurs, but a higher value honeypot offers much more information about the nature of the interaction.

If you've fully considered what the attacker sees, what the attacker thinks, and what the attacker does . . . you're likely to trick them into falling for your traps and alerting you to their presence.

Case Study

Let's apply the deception planning methodology to a single network through a case study.

You work at a medium-size food company that produces delicious chicken noodle and tomato soup[5]. While all located in the same region, SoupCorp manufactures each variety of soup in a separate plant. The company also has a headquarters office building and a distribution warehouse where soup is transported and repackaged before being shipped out to retailers.

Figure 3-7 shows the layout of the network, along with honeypot deployment locations.

---

[5] I'm more of a potato-leek soup kind of guy, but it's not my company.

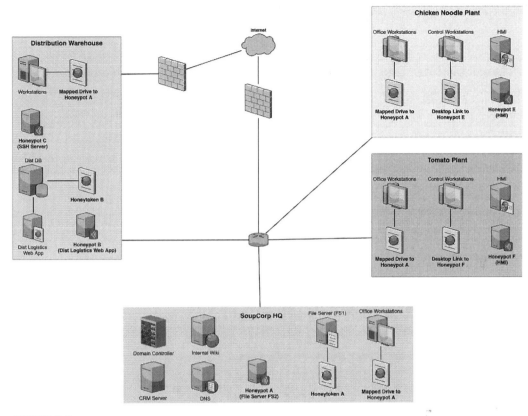

FIGURE 3-7:

SoupCorp Network Diagram

Let's break down these honeypots and their placement based on the See-Think-Do Deception Methodology.

Honeypot A: File Server

SoupCorp has a file server named FS1 in the HQ network that users across the organization access to edit and view essential files. Most user workstations have multiple drives mapped to shared folders on this server, including a HOME (H) drive, a PRODUCTION (I) drive, and a FILES (J) drive. The file server is visible throughout the network since it is accessible in most places. Honeypot A is a honey system deployed using OpenCanary to mimic the file server. It's placed on the same network segment as the file server, and user workstations have network drives mapped to it. There is no reason for a typical network user to ever deliberately connect to or access Honeypot A.

The attacker *sees* this honey system if:

- They scan the file server network range from any network location
- They view the mapped drives on any user workstation

The attacker *thinks* the honey system is valuable because it blends in with functionality provided by the legitimate file server. It shares the following characteristics with the legitimate file server:

- Exists in contiguous IP space
- Has a similar name (FS2)
- Responds to operating system identification probes in a similar manner
- Contains similarly named shared folders
- Drives mapped to it from workstations are named DATA (K)

The attacker *does* something that alerts you to their presence when they:

- Scan the honeypot from another system they control in your network
- Browse to the mapped drive from a user workstation

Honeypot B: Distribution Logistics Web App

Staff in the distribution warehouse use a web application to manage the logistics of moving soup from the plant locations to retailers. The app is only accessible from devices connected to the warehouse network. Honeypot B is a honey service deployed using Microsoft IIS to mimic the web application. It provides a login screen that mirrors the legitimate web application and accepts credentials, but will never authenticate a user.

The attacker *sees* this honey service if they scan the warehouse network from a device connected to it.

The attacker *thinks* the honey service is valuable because it blends in with functionality provided by the legitimate web application. They share the following characteristics:

- Exists in contiguous IP space
- Has a similar name
- Uses the same web server platform
- Hosts a visually identical website

The attacker *does* something that alerts you to their presence when they:

- Scan the honeypot from another system they control in your network
- Connect to the web server to view the home page
- Attempt to log into the web site

Honeypot C: SSH Server

The SoupCorp network is primarily Windows-based with a few Linux servers. The distribution warehouse doesn't contain any Windows servers at all but does possess valuable information in the logistics database accessed via the logistics web application. Honeypot C is a honey service deployed using Cowrie to mimic a Linux SSH server. It provides a login prompt, a set of guessable credentials that will allow access, and a fake Linux file system available after authentication.

The attacker *sees* the honey service if they scan the warehouse network from a device connected to it. This visibility ensures the honeypot appears in the same scans that also reveal valuable assets like the warehouse web and database servers.

The attacker *thinks* the honey service is valuable because it stands out and is entirely different from other systems and services that will appear in scan results. Its unique characteristics include:

- Responding to probes using the profile of an Ubuntu Linux system
- Advertising port 22 open with an SSH banner
- Using the server name BISQUE

The attacker *does* something that alerts you to their presence when they:

- Scan the honeypot from another system they control in your network
- Connect to the honeypot using an SSH client
- Attempt to authenticate to the honeypot using an SSH client

Honeypot D and E: Human-Machine Interface

The plant networks leverage industrial control systems (ICS) and a human-machine interface (HMI) to monitor the production line. Administrators configured dedicated workstations to automatically open the HMI web interface in a browser window upon startup, which is the only application workers use. The desktop contains an icon named SOUPHMI that opens the web browser link to the HMI. The plant HMIs are only accessible from these workstations due to host-based firewall restrictions. Honeypots D and E are honey services deployed at each plant network using netcat to mimic an HTTP server. The HMI interface is complex, so the honeypot simply accepts HTTP connections without providing content in response. Another icon named SOUPHMI2 is placed on the desktop of plant control workstations, pointing to the honeypot. Managers instruct employees never to use it.

The attacker *sees* the honey service if they gain access to a control workstation and scan the network or find the SOUPHMI2 icon on the desktop.

The attacker *thinks* the honey service is valuable because it blends in with the legitimate HMI link on the control workstation desktop and provides similar responses to network-based probes. They'll share the following characteristics:

- Exist in contiguous IP space
- Has a similar name
- Has the same open ports
- Has the same HTTP server banner
- Uses the same naming structure and icon as the legitimate HMI link

The attacker *does* something that alerts you to their presence when they:

- Scan the honeypot from a control workstation they've compromised
- Access the URL linked from the desktop icon present on control workstations

Honey Token A: File Server Document

SoupCorp stores sensitive information on the HQ file server FS1. This data includes information about suppliers, manufacturing processes, soup formulas, and customers. Most users have some access to various shared folders on the system that access FS1. So, Honey token A is a Microsoft Excel document placed in shared folders that contain sensitive information. The document is named "NEW RECIPE DATA.xlsx" but provides no real information of value.

The attacker *sees* the honey token if they compromise a system used by someone who accesses the file server and has mapped drives or links to shared folders on it. It is visible from most common footholds in the network.

The attacker *thinks* the honey token is an interesting file because of the characteristics that make it stand out from other files. These characteristics include:

- A name in all caps, while other files are lower or camel-cased
- Being an Excel file amongst mostly word documents
- An enticing name
- A recent "last updated" date

The attacker *does* something that alerts you to their presence when they:

- Open the file
- Copy or move the file

Honey Token B: Distribution Database Record

The previously mentioned distribution web app stores information in a database that resides on a separate server. Honey token B is a database table named USERS that the web server doesn't utilize as part of normal operations. The users table contains only false user information.

The attacker *sees* the honey token if they can enumerate the database directly outside the normal context of the web application, either by performing a SQL injection attack on the web server or compromising the database server directly.

The attacker *thinks* the USERS table is valuable because it mimics the name of a table that could contain username and password information.

The attacker *does* something that alerts you to their presence when they:

- Execute a query that returns the USERS table
- Attempt to log into another system with a username obtained from the USERS table

The SoupCorp case study doesn't encompass every possible honeypot you could create based on the network diagram in Figure 3-7. Still, it does highlight a few that are likely to be successful in the event of a compromise. You can take this exercise farther by applying the See-Think-Do Deception framework to come up with other honeypot ideas based on the network layout.

Conclusion

I hope this chapter has helped you understand that it isn't just the software you use for honeypotting that matters, but more importantly, the context in which you deploy it. If you only deploy honeypots without thought to their placement and what they mimic, then you'll probably miss some detection opportunities. It's the combination of honeypot technology, its placement, what it mimics, and the level of interaction it provides that determine the deception strategy, and eventually, the success of the detection mechanism as a whole.

Now that you know how to plan for honeypots and where to place them, we'll talk about monitoring them next.

LOGGING AND MONITORING

IF AN ATTACKER INTERACTS WITH A HONEYPOT, BUT that interaction isn't logged and brought to the attention of an analyst, did it happen? Of course it did, but it won't help you catch the bad guy. Your honeypot deployment isn't complete until you've planned the logging and monitoring infrastructure that supports its goal.

Logging and Monitoring (L&M) is a function of Network Security Monitoring (NSM). Specifically, it describes the hardware and software infrastructure that collects and stores evidence used for alerting analysts to the presence of an attacker, and supporting their investigation of the attack. Both L&M and NSM are broad subjects that could easily warrant their own books, so I can't cover them in full detail here. However, because honeypot-based detection is a subset of NSM, it's critical to touch on essential parts that will make your honeypot deployment successful. In this chapter, I'll give an overview of logging and monitoring mechanisms useful for capturing the interaction between attackers and honeypots.

Interaction Logging and Monitoring Tools

If you've done everything right so far and your honeypot is visible, appears to provide value, and provides a meaningful response to a stimulus, then an attacker who has gained access to your network will likely interact with it. A *honeypot interaction* is the crucial event logged when an attacker sends a stimulus to the honeypot. This is the moment you've been waiting for; it's the honeypot's time to shine. The nature of the event varies based on the type of honeypot.

For honey system interactions, key events could be:

- Establishing a TCP session
- Probing UDP ports
- Probing ICMP ports

For honey service interactions, key events could be:

- For a web server, browsing to the home page
- For an RDP server, attempting to log into the system
- For a file server, accessing a shared folder
- For an SNMP server, querying information
- For a DHCP server, requesting an address

For honey token interactions, key events could be:

- Opening, copying, moving, or deleting a file
- Enumerating a table database
- Logging into a system with a specific set of credentials

While these are only a few of many potential examples, for a honeypot to be useful it must provide or be paired with a mechanism to log these interactions so that you'll know they happened. Whenever a log matches specific criteria and a system[1] brings it to the attention of an analyst, it becomes an *alert*. The distinction here is important! All alerts are also logs, but only some logs are alerts (Figure 4-1). A log becomes an alert when a notification occurs and there is an expected response. An alert is an actionable event that launches an investigation by one or more analysts. Even if the alert only points to other log entries, it still contains its own timestamp and metadata, making it a log entry itself.

---

[1] This is often an Intrusion Detection System (IDS), but it might also be a function of some other component of logging and monitoring infrastructure.

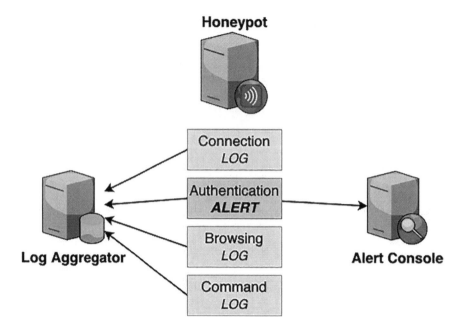

FIGURE 4-1:

This honeypot sends all events to the log aggregator, but only events that launch an investigation go to the alert console as well.

How you choose to receive honeypot logs and alerts should align with how you're already consuming these data types in your organization. There are several tools at your disposal, and they make up what we'll collectively refer to as a Logging and Monitoring (L&M) infrastructure:

Email Alerts: Alert notifications sent directly to an individual analyst or group of analysts subscribed to a distribution list. Starting investigations with email alerts is convenient because it allows for quick communication among concerned parties in a single thread. This mechanism doesn't scale up well but serves as the most common alerting mechanism for small organizations or those without another alerting console. Larger organizations may still choose email for their highest priority alerts.

Text Message Alerts: Alert notifications are sent to analysts by SMS. Most people don't stray far from their phones and are unlikely to miss a text[2]. You might not want to share sensitive information in the alert since many phones are often unmanaged personal devices. That may make communicating the seriousness of the event difficult when

---

[2] Boundaries are good. If you're a manager, don't overwhelm your employees with text alerts. Not every analyst needs the distraction of knowing THAT salesperson downloaded another malware toolbar right as they're about to sit down to dinner with family.

limited by this format. SMS is also space constrained, so most text alerts will probably just include a simple overview and a link for more information.

Chat Message Alerts: Alert notifications are sent to analysts in a shared analyst chat room using tools like Slack, Discord, or Microsoft Teams. These messages place the alert into a mechanism built for collaboration, making it easy for analysts to begin a discussion around the investigation. Because chat can move fast, this is best for smaller organizations or when limited to only higher priority and lower volume alerting.

APIs or Webhooks: An Application Programming Interface (API) is intermediary software that receives requests and provides it to another application. For example, a SIEM may provide an API for power users to interact with alerts. This allows for programmatic integration with the SIEM without the limitations its interface imposes. A webhook provides similar functionality but relies on the HTTP protocol for data formatting and transmission while monitoring for changes based on predefined rules, rather than relying on polling[3]. Both APIs and webhooks provide tremendous flexibility for integrations with other tools. However, those other tools must support the functionality and you may have to write your own code to interact with the interfaces properly.

Alert Consoles: A centralized console that displays alerts from multiple sources is the most common way analysts receive alerts. A true alert console shows you alerts in a queue while also allowing you to assign a status to them, like open, in progress, or closed. Only open or in progress alerts are typically shown in the console, serving as a checklist of alerts pending analyst review. Consoles usually archive closed alerts for historical searching. Alert consoles also typically provide mechanisms for distinguishing more critical events, either by categorization or through a conduit to other notification mechanisms (like email or text message). More advanced alert consoles allow you to create multiple views based on specific criteria, like a unique console exclusively for honeypot-based alerts. Free options like TheHive, Squert, or OSSIM are prevalent along with commercial offerings built into SIEM tools.

Log Aggregators: A log aggregator indexes logs in a central location for you to search through them. Log aggregators differ from alert consoles because they merely allow you to view alert logs without creating a queue to assign a status to them. That's to say that they treat alert logs like any other logs. They also don't come with the ability to elevate the importance of critical events or assign priority to individual logs. Most organizations use log aggregators in conjunction with alert consoles, and some SIEM solutions serve both purposes. Popular options include Elastic Stack or Splunk.

---

[3] For a more detailed description of the differences between APIs and Webhooks, see https://www.craftersoftware.com/blog/2019/08/webhooks-vs-apis--whats-the-difference.

SIEM: Security Information and Event Management (SIEM) tools combine one or more of the previously described functions along with other features like collaboration and reporting. The definition and capability of SIEM varies between vendors but most often include a log aggregation and alert console functionality together. While this allows your logging and monitoring infrastructure to exist in a single ecosystem, the tools come with an extensive configuration and maintenance overhead. They're also quite pricey. Common SIEM platforms include LogRhythm and QRadar.

Honeypot-based alerts generally have a low false positive rate once you've allow-listed noisy legitimate activity. Alert consoles should display these higher-quality alerts more prominently than alerts from traditional sources with higher false positive rates. Achieving this may mean giving honeypot-based alerts a higher priority within your alert console, sending them to a separate console, or leveraging email and text alerts where you otherwise wouldn't.

Some honeypots support alerting directly using a few of these mechanisms. Still, for the most part, you'll probably rely on the honeypot logging notable events to disk or sending them over the network in a standard log transport format. In other instances, the honeypot itself won't provide logging at all and you'll rely on auditing mechanisms offered by the operating system or network sensors. In either case, you'll have to rely on additional technology to feed the logs into a tool that provides the alert notification you desire. I often refer to the mechanisms that connect all these things as the plumbing, just like water distribution pipes in a house.

Plumbing Logs

The logs generated during honeypot interaction are only valuable if they're made available to analysts who can use them to launch or further an investigation. That typically means getting them to one of the notification mechanisms listed above, but few honeypots have a native capability to do that by themselves. Most honeypots write log entries to disk because it's the easiest way to store their output. There are several ways to ship these logs to their final destination, and you'll be limited by whatever technology is on the receiving end. You should fully comprehend the information provided by the log source and the requirements of the destination that you hope to ingest those logs. I use the log plumbing reference framework in Figure 4-2 to help plan L&M infrastructure.

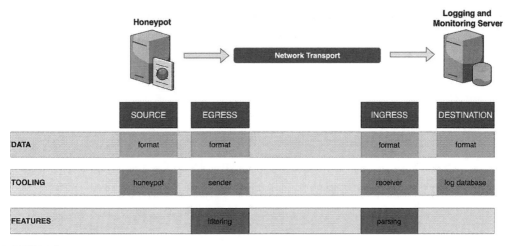

FIGURE 4-2:

A log plumbing reference framework for logging and monitoring infrastructure

The logging and monitoring architecture framework provides an overview of the plumbing mechanisms used to ship logs from the honeypot on the left to an L&M server on the right. The four columns represent the sequential phases of log transport:

- Source: How the data is generated at its origin
- Egress: How the data is transmitted from its origin
- Ingress: How the data is received at its destination
- Destination: How the data is stored at its destination

The three rows represent the characteristics and handling of the data.

- Data: The format the data exists in
- Tooling: The software tools used to generate, manipulate, transmit, or store the data
- Features: Unique transformations applied to the data

Plumbing L&M infrastructure is not unlike plumbing a house. For the most part, you should use the same size and type of pipes everywhere. You can change both of these things, but you have to use the right adapters and adhesives, or you'll end up with a mess. Sources and destinations dictate most of your plumbing. Your toilet only has one water input, so you must eventually configure the piping between the inflow to your house and the toilet to match with the available connection.

Similarly, log plumbing is also all about compatibility with sources and destinations dictating many of the components. A honeypot only outputs logs in a specific format, and your destination L&M platform only accepts logs in specific formats. If those formats are not the same, you'll have to manipulate the data during one of the four phases shown in the L&M reference framework.

There are five essential questions to ask when planning L&M infrastructure:

1. What log formats does the honeypot provide?
2. What log formats does my L&M server accept?
3. What tool will I use to send logs over the network from my honeypot?
4. What tool will I use to receive the logs sent to the L&M server?
5. How will I filter and parse the honeypot logs for useful analysis?

Let's discuss each of these in more depth.

What log formats does the honeypot provide?

Most honeypots that you'll build or deploy (and many of them mentioned in this book) write evidence of interaction to text-based logs stored on the hard drive. They'll typically use a standardized logging format like CEF or Syslog, or a custom format prescribed by the developer. These are most often single files with one log entry per line but can also be multiline logs like JSON. Below, I have several examples of the same log entry representing authentication to a Cowrie SSH honeypot. However, notice the differences in each log representation:

Cowrie Default:
```
2020-05-06T16:08:46.452021Z [SSHService b'ssh-userauth' on
HoneyPotSSHTransport,1,172.16.16.212] login attempt [b'sanders'/
b'gotcha'] succeeded
```

JSON:
```
{"eventid":"cowrie.login.
success","username":"sanders","password":"gotcha","message":"login
attempt [sanders/gotcha] succeeded","sensor":"idh","timestamp":"2020-05-
06T16:08:46.452021Z","src_ip":"172.16.16.212","session":"7eff6e5815e4"}
```

CEF:
```
2020-05-06T16:08:46.452021Z CEF:0|Cowrie|Cowrie|1.0|cowrie.login.
success|cowrie.login.success|5|app=SSHv2 destinationServicename=sshd
deviceExternalId=idh msg=login attempt [sanders/gotcha] succeeded
src=172.16.16.212 proto=tcp duser=sanders outcome=success
```

Syslog:
```
May  6 16:08:46 idh cowrie: [SSHService b'ssh-userauth' on
HoneyPotSSHTransport,1,172.16.16.212] login attempt [sanders/gotcha]
succeeded
```

Where honeypots don't provide their own logs, you'll rely on other auditing mechanisms. For example, the honey documents I'll describe in Chapter 7 rely on

Windows Event Logging. In the same chapter, the honey folders I'll walk you through rely on intercepting DNS requests, either through host logs or capturing network traffic.

What log formats does my L&M server accept?

Just like the honeypot only provides so many log formats at the source, the final destination of your logs only supports a limited number of formats as well. Most L&M platform developers know that they'll be getting data from a wide variety of sources, so you'll usually find flexibility in the types of inputs here.

What tool will I use to send logs over the network from the honeypot?

You'll need a mechanism to transmit honeypot logs from the source to the receiver on the L&M server. The sender must be able to read the logs generated by the honeypot. The sender may also convert the logs to the required format of the final destination, although tools usually do that on the receiver side. Since you're moving data, you must also consider the reliability of that transport and the security of the data in transit through encryption. Common senders include flexible open source tools like syslog-ng, rsyslog, and nxlog, as well as proprietary senders designed to work with specific receiver platforms such as the Splunk Universal Forwarder, Elastic Beats, and Windows Event Forwarding (WEF).

What tool will I use to receive logs sent to the L&M server?

You'll need a mechanism to receive the logs transmitted by the sender and place them in the log server database. The receiver might also be asked to convert the logs into an acceptable format for the destination. Some L&M platforms provide built-in receivers. For example, Elasticsearch can receive data directly from the network, and Splunk has a wide array of network-based input options, including a syslog receiver. Some receivers pair well with specific senders, such as Windows Event Collector (WEC) receiving logs from Windows Event Forwarding (WEF)[4].

How will I filter and parse the honeypot logs for effective analysis?

If you've answered the four previous questions, then you technically have the tools you need to ship your logs to a place where you can analyze them. However, you're not done yet. First, consider that some honeypots are excessively noisy and that others add their logs to existing operating system log files like the Linux messages log. Instead of wasting

---

[4] WEF/WEC deserves more attention than I can give it in this book. It's a simple, useful way to ship event logs around your network from Windows hosts. Learn more about it at https://docs.microsoft.com/en-us/windows/security/threat-protection/use-windows-event-forwarding-to-assist-in-intrusion-detection.

resources transmitting, processing, and storing those logs, you should filter them by disregarding logs that won't have investigative or alerting value. For example, you might not want to audit every time someone connects to a honeypot, but rather, only when they authenticate to it. So, you'll filter out logged connection attempts and only keep the authentication attempts. You'll also rely on this filtering ability as you allow-list users and hosts that need to periodically communicate with your honeypots, like authorized scanners or network inventory tools.

You can filter data at the source or destination, but it's more resource efficient when it occurs at the source because it saves the bandwidth and processing required to transmit the log across the network. However, disregarding those events means they're gone forever. Filtering logs should be a thoughtful and deliberate exercise where you carefully consider the value of the data.

After filtering, you must consider the investigative value of the logs. Logs are more useful when they are easily searchable, and that often means parsing specific values into unique fields. For example, start by looking at the unparsed Elastic Stack log in Figure 4-3.

Time ⌄	message
May 7, 2020 @ 13:39:00.004	1500479094 1366 192.168.0.188 TCP_MISS/200 12851 GET http://www.bing.com/search? DIRECT/122.160.242.147 text/html

FIGURE 4-3:

An unparsed log in Elastic Stack

All the data is there, so you can search for this log in its unparsed state. If I search for 122.160.242.147, this log shows up in the results. But what if I want to perform more advanced searches? For one, searching for the range 122.160.242.0/24 wouldn't identify this log. Similarly, if I want to identify every unique IP address that appears in my honeypot logs and sort that list by the number of occurrences, I can't do that either. Both of those scenarios require the IP address to be parsed into its own field and identified as a specific type, shown in Figure 4-4.

Time ⌄	srcip	dstip	url	content_type	bytes_xferred
Jul 19, 2017 @ 15:44:54.000	192.168.0.188	122.160.242.147	http://www.bing.com/search?	text/html	12,851

FIGURE 4-4:

A parsed log in Elastic Stack

With individual fields identified and typed, I'm free to conduct more complex searches, incorporate data into visualizations, and perform statistical analysis through techniques like frequency analysis[5].

You can parse data at the source, but it most commonly occurs at the destination since the L&M platform usually dictates the format.

Logging Pipeline Examples

It's impossible to cover every potential logging pipeline configuration, but I'll walk through a few examples here, so you'll grasp how to conceptualize this process. I'll briefly cover a couple of common logging technologies as well, but you'll need to conduct some independent research for specific resources on installing and configuring these tools. Later in the book, I'll describe the logging facility of each honeypot I discuss so that you can figure out how it best fits into your existing L&M strategy.

Syslog-ng to Remote Syslog-ng

The first example I'll describe places us on a network with a Cowrie SSH honeypot that logs authentication attempts. Cowrie is configured to write logs in syslog format to /var/log/syslog. This organization doesn't yet have any dedicated L&M infrastructure, but we still want to transport the honeypot logs to a centralized file server for safe-keeping and ease of analysis. I've depicted the logging pipeline in Figure 4-5.

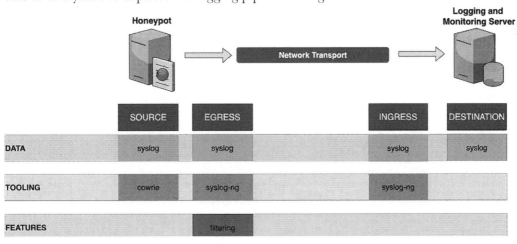

FIGURE 4-5:

Cowrie to Generic File Server via Syslog-ng

---

[5] Often called aggregations or stacking, this technique is one of the most useful data analysis techniques within investigations and threat hunting.

Source

I've configured Cowrie to write syslog-formatted logs into a file at /var/log/hpot/auth.log[6]. The log entries look like this:

```
May 22 11:27:05 hpot1 cowrie: [cowrie.ssh.factory.CowrieSSHFactory]
New connection: 192.168.61.1:60556 (192.168.61.132:2222) [session:
103e41131570]
May 22 11:27:05 hpot1 cowrie: [HoneyPotSSHTransport,2,192.168.61.1]
Remote SSH version: SSH-2.0-OpenSSH_7.6
May 22 11:27:12 hpot1 cowrie: [SSHService 'ssh-userauth' on
HoneyPotSSHTransport,2,192.168.61.1] login attempt [sanders/password]
failed
```

The file contains data from other inputs, so it must be filtered before it reaches the destination.

Egress

I'll ship the data over the network using syslog-ng[7], a tool well-equipped to move syslog data around. It can also filter the logs, which is great because we don't want to send the entire contents of auth.log to the destination. This syslog-ng config identifies the source of the logs, filters them for the program string "cowrie," and sends them to a central log server at 192.168.1.5 over the network using the TCP transport protocol:

```
# defines the source file
source s_hpot1 { file("/var/log/hpot/auth.log"); };

# defines the remote ingress
destination d_fileserver { network("192.168.1.5" transport("tcp")); };

# filters unwanted logs
filter f_cowrie { program(cowrie); };

# connects the source, filter, and destination
log { source(s_hpot1); filter(f_cowrie); destination(d_fileserver); };
```

Ingress

Once the log data reaches the final destination, I'll simply write it into a file. Syslog-ng can receive the data over the network and write the file, so we'll use it on the ingress side

---

[6] You'll learn more about Cowrie logging in Chapter 6.

[7] Learn more about open source syslog-ng and its configuration here: https://www.syslog-ng.com/technical-documents/list/syslog-ng-open-source-edition/

too. This config identifies the honeypot log source as 192.168.1.100, opens TCP port 5514 to receive the data, and writes it to /var/log/cowrie.log:

```
# defines the network source
source s_hpot1 {tcp(ip(192.168.1.100) port(5514)); };

# defines the local file to store the incoming logs
destination d_cowrie { file("/var/log/cowrie.log"); };

# connects the source and destination
log { source(s_hpot1); destination(d_cowrie); };
```

Destination

The data now exists on the destination server in the same form as it did at the source, but in a dedicated file. You can search these logs using Linux command line tools or with any text editor or spreadsheet tool.

This logging pipeline represents about as simple as moving logs around can get. This setup wouldn't be feasible for many data sources due to volume, but because honeypots are such a low volume, this strategy isn't unreasonable. Of course, there are other considerations to keep in mind, such as log file rotation at the destination and alerting when new honeypot logs appear.

Syslog-ng to Remote Log Management

The second example I'll describe relies on Basic Auth Pot (BAP), a simple service honeypot that creates a web server that prompts a visiting user for a username and password using HTTP basic authentication[8]. Like many honeypots, BAP writes the results of the interaction to a custom text-based log with a new line for every log entry. In this scenario, the organization I'm working with centralizes security-related logs in an Elasticsearch database as part of the Elastic Stack[9]. I illustrated the logging pipeline in Figure 4-6.

---

[8] I don't cover BAP elsewhere in this book, but you can learn about it here: https://github.com/bjeborn/basic-auth-pot.

[9] Learn about Elastic Stack here at https://elastic.co. If you want to go farther, take my online ELK course here: http://networkdefense.co/courses/elk.

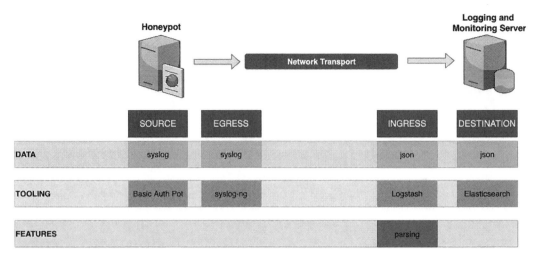

Honeypot | Logging and Monitoring Server

Network Transport

	SOURCE	EGRESS		INGRESS	DESTINATION
DATA	syslog	syslog		json	json
TOOLING	Basic Auth Pot	syslog-ng		Logstash	Elasticsearch
FEATURES				parsing	

FIGURE 4-6:

Basic Auth Pot to ELK with help from Syslog-ng and Logstash

Sources

BAP writes data to a text file in a custom format. The log entries look like this:

```
Starting bap on 172.16.16.151:8080
[2020-05-07 10:37:11,072] 172.16.16.212:53861 Basic admin:nope
[2020-05-07 10:46:36,494] 172.16.16.212:54177 Basic admin:admin
[2020-05-07 10:46:39,185] 172.16.16.212:54178 Basic sanders:gotcha
```

As you can see, the log file contains interaction logs we want (lines 2 through 4) and operational logs we don't care about (line 1). I'll filter and parse the unwanted logs at ingress in this example since we'll leverage some of Logstash's robust parsing capabilities for filtering.

Egress

Moving text-based logs is quite simple with syslog-ng, so we'll stick with that method here. This configuration identifies the source of the logs at /opt/bap/bap.log and sends them to 172.16.16.192 over the network using the TCP transport protocol:

```
# defines the source file
source s_hpot1 { file("/opt/bap/bap.log"); };

# defines the remote ingress
destination d_elastic { network("172.16.16.192" transport("tcp")); };

# connects the source and destination
log { source(s_hpot1); destination(d_elastic); };
```

Ingress

Unlike the last scenario, this organization has a proper log aggregator to store these logs. We're shipping logs to Elasticsearch, which stores data as JSON documents. That means I'll need to convert the custom BAP text logs into JSON format before I can insert them into the log database. Logstash is an excellent choice for this task because it's part of the Elastic Stack already. It can receive input from syslog-ng, parse the data into fields, filter unwanted data, and store the data in JSON format in Elasticsearch.

The Logstash configuration that accomplishes this task is shown in Figure 4-7.

```
input {
    syslog {
        port => 5514     ❶
    }
}

filter {
    grok {
        match => { message => "%{INT:year}\-%{INT:month}-%{INT:day}
%{TIME:time}] %{IPV4:srcip}:%{INT:srcport} %{WORD:auth}     ❷
%{WORD:username}:%{WORD:password}"}
    }

      mutate {
  ❸      remove_fields => ["year", "month", "day", "time", "message"]
    }

      if "_grokparsefailure" in [tags] {
  ❹      drop { }
    }
}

output {
        elasticsearch { hosts => ['localhost:9200']
        index => "bap" }
  ❺
      if [username] == "sanders" {
            elasticsearch { hosts => ['localhost:9200']
            index => "alerts" }
    }
}
```

FIGURE 4-7:

This Logstash config ingests and parses BAP logs on ingress

Let's break this down:

1. The input section uses the Logstash syslog plugin to create a listener for network data sent over port 5514.
2. In the filter block, the grok plugin matches the interaction logs using a regular-expression-like syntax and parses them into individual fields.
3. The mutate plugin drops fields we don't care about. We're removing the date and time information because we're already getting that from the

syslog header appended to the log at the time of egress.

4. Any logs that don't match the grok pattern have the value *grokparsefailure* added to the tags field of the record, so I use the presence of that value to drop any logs that don't match the pattern. This tactic ensures the operational logs we don't care about don't make their way to the database.

5. In the output block, Logstash sends all the parsed BAP logs to the bap index. Logstash also sends authentication attempts matching the username *sanders* to a dedicated alerts index. I've done this because *sanders* is a high-value account. Concern that an attacker might have stolen this user's credentials warrants more immediate alerting. Presumably, the alerts index feeds a higher priority analyst work queue.

Destination

Each log now exists in a JSON document in the Elasticsearch database. You can search logs using the Elasticsearch REST APIs, through a web-based tool like Kibana (also part of the Elastic Stack), or through Elastalert which periodically executes queries and notifies you about new matches. Figure 4-8 shows a BAP log queried from Elasticsearch through the Kibana interface. At the top, you can see the log in a format that's easier to visually parse, and below is the log in its raw JSON format. Notice that the document contains data from the log along with additional metadata added by Elasticsearch.

FIGURE 4-8:

BAP honeypot activity in Kibana

This logging pipeline is similar to something you could encounter in a real organization where you're integrating your honeypot logs into an existing L&M solution.

Additional L&M Considerations

The two scenarios I've described here might not fit your exact L&M infrastructure, but I hope that you'll be able to apply the log plumbing reference framework to whatever components you have to work with. L&M is a broad subject to which authors have dedicated entire books, so there's no way for me to cover it adequately here. But I will mention a few other considerations as you think about your honeypot logs and plumbing them to an accessible location.

Encryption in Transit

The default option for most log transport tools (including syslog-ng that I used in the earlier example) sends data unencrypted. Anyone on your network with the ability to install a packet capture utility and perform ARP cache poisoning or any other man-in-the-middle attack could theoretically intercept and read that data. Honeypot logs constitute sensitive data because they contain information about critical network assets, and they may reveal that a system is a honeypot before the attacker has interacted with the device. Additionally, these logs could show that an attacker breached the organization to someone who shouldn't know that yet, whether that's another attacker, an auditor, or an employee. You should always take steps to encrypt honeypot logs and alerts in transit. Most log transport tools provide encryption functionality, but you may have to configure it yourself since it often won't be enabled by default.

Access Control

Just like you should protect honeypot logs in transit, you should also protect them at rest. You should tightly control access to your L&M database, only providing access to security analysts who need access to logs for investigations. You should also consider access compartmentalization. If analysts can view the logs with an L&M platform web interface, most of them probably only need access to that tool rather than administrative access to the system hosting it. Also, remember that not enough access can be nearly as detrimental as too much. If analysts can't appropriately interact with and manipulate logs, you may wind up missing a compromise. You should protect honeypot log data, but don't silo it away from the people who need it.

Complex Logging Infrastructure

The examples I walked through all involved a log-generating source transmitting directly to a log-receiving destination. Most small or simple networks work that way, but more extensive networks often require additional technology to handle their diversity and scale. These concerns might include:

- Using log forwarders to aggregate logs from one physical location and sending them to a destination network segment
- Using load balancers to control the flow of logs coming to a single destination
- Routing logs to different locations based on their source or other characteristics

Many of the tools I've mentioned can handle these scenarios, but it'll require a more complex configuration and a better understanding of how the tool works.

Log Backup

The only thing worse than getting attacked is getting attacked and having your logging platform fail or seeing it wiped by an attacker who gains access to that system. Logs are critical data, so they should be treated accordingly and backed up. Some commercial L&M platforms provide built-in backup to a secondary appliance (often for an additional cost), while organizations using free platforms may create two instances and send the logs to both locations from the same source or forwarder.

Monitoring Up/Down Status

When you spend so much time thinking about monitoring your network, it's easy to forget about monitoring the software that does the monitoring[10]. You or your network and systems operation teams probably have software used to monitor the up/down status of critical systems like domain controllers, routers, and application servers. You should extend these mechanisms to honeypots and the L&M platforms that receive their logs. Finding out you've missed a breach because your honeypot crashed is a dreadful experience. You can accomplish this oversight by using service monitoring tools to notify you when honeypot services go down. Another technique is sending synthetic interactions to honeypots at regular intervals. Filter these events from the analyst alerting console, but generate alerts to engineers when a honeypot fails to generate a scheduled event.

---

[10] How does that old saying go? Who will log the loggers?

Be Mindful of Data Abstraction

I've discussed making data more easily searchable by parsing it into specific fields and types. While this is a great practice, you should be familiar with the transformation taking place behind the scenes. One time, I discovered a signature I had written for a specific URL pattern in proxy data had failed to catch something it should have matched. After a lot of frustration, I found out that one of the engineers responsible for filtering the proxy data had configured the data source to render some URL encoded characters in an unexpected way prior to ingesting the logs into the log aggregator. This meant that my signature was doomed from the start because I wasn't aware of how the data was manipulated before my interaction point.

An analyst who only examines parsed data without understanding the raw data format will be forced to make assumptions about how tools are interpreting the data. Those assumptions might lead to some poor decision-making. It's a good idea to regularly audit your data sources and ensure they adhere to a consistent and predictable data model.

Conclusion

In this chapter, I described a reference framework for planning L&M infrastructure and several of the considerations surrounding it and technologies that can support it. As I describe specific honeypot technology later in the book, I'll elaborate on their logging capability so you can plug them into the log plumbing reference framework and plan how to fit them into whatever logging infrastructure you're working with.

BUILDING YOUR FIRST HONEYPOT FROM SCRATCH

YOU SHOULD NOW HAVE THE CONCEPTUAL
knowledge you need to plan a honeypot deployment and the logging
infrastructure that supports it. Now, it's time to learn about the actual
software you'll use for the honeypots themselves. Starting with this
chapter, I'll dive into examples of honeypot solutions that you can
leverage on your network. The best honeypot is the simplest, so we'll
start as simple as we can by building your own service honeypots using
netcat. There are more robust honeypot solutions available, but this
example demonstrates the simplicity that can constitute an effective
honeypot.

Netcat

Netcat is an application that sends and receives data over a network using TCP/IP
protocols. That may sound very broad, but that's why netcat earned the nickname "The
TCP/IP Swiss Army Knife." It has a tremendous number of uses. You can use netcat to:

- Send and receive arbitrary data over the network
- Relay data from one host to another

- Port scan a range of hosts
- Redirect data from an incoming port to another port
- Proxy connections between hosts
- Create a minimalistic chat client
- Shovel commands through a backdoor on a compromised system

Netcat has been around since 1996. Since then, it's gone through many enhancements and been forked into other projects. You can find netcat versions that work on most platforms, including Linux, Windows, and macOS. The extensive usage of netcat is beneficial because there are tons of examples and support a mere Google search away. But, the splintering of the original code base and the variety in supported features means that you may eventually run into headaches if you try to execute a trusty go-to netcat function on a new platform that uses a slightly modified version of the tool.

Netcat is also very portable. It's small and typically contained within a single executable that makes it easy to use directly or embed it into other tools. You'll find netcat integrated into commercial tools and malicious binaries alike. Attackers have used netcat for malicious purposes so frequently that many antivirus applications will detect and attempt to quarantine it. Rest soundly though; if you've acquired netcat from a trusted source, then you shouldn't have anything to worry about. The tool is legitimate, but like many tools, adversaries can use it for malicious purposes.

Your operating system may come with a version of netcat installed. For the examples in this book, I'll rely on ncat, a version of Netcat created by the same people who maintain the Nmap scanning utility. You can download it directly from **https://nmap.org/ ncat** or install it using a package manager, like apt on Ubuntu:

```
sudo apt-get install ncat
```

If the ncat isn't available as an APTT package on your version of Linux, it's also included with the more ubiquitous nmap package[1]:

```
sudo apt-get install nmap
```

Make sure you installed netcat successfully by running the command `ncat - version`, as shown in Figure 5-1.

---

[1] The screenshots in this chapter are shown using a macOS terminal connected to an Ubuntu 18 host.

```
● ● ●                sanders — sanders@hpot1: ~ — ssh 172.16.16.151 — 44×5
[sanders@hpot1:~$ ncat --version
Ncat: Version 7.01 ( https://nmap.org/ncat )
sanders@hpot1:~$
```

FIGURE 5-1:

Ncat output

We'll use netcat to construct a couple of very simple honeypots in this chapter.

A Telnet Netcat Honeypot

The first example I'll walk you through is a simple telnet honeypot. Telnet is a protocol used for bidirectional text-based communication between two network devices. It allows for the creation of a virtual terminal and can facilitate authentication. At one point, telnet was the primary mechanism enabling users to access and interact with systems and network devices. People gravitated towards telnet because of its simplicity and ease of implementation. However, this same simplicity also left it without important features like encryption of data in transit. For this reason and a few others, telnet eventually fell out of favor and has mostly been replaced with more secure protocols like SSH. Of course, plenty of legacy telnet equipment still exists.

Telnet is a good candidate for a honey service because it stands out. Most attackers have a keen eye for spotting legacy services and protocols. Someone who encounters a system with the default telnet port (23) open will almost certainly try to connect to it. At a minimum, they may just grab the banner advertised by the system, or they may go farther and attempt to log in to it by guessing default credentials or using stolen credentials. Let's use netcat to build a telnet honeypot that will capture some of this interaction.

Netcat has two modes: sending or listening. We'll mostly rely on the listening function to create the telnet honeypot shown in Figure 5-2.

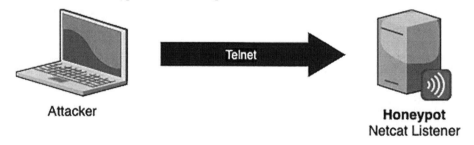

FIGURE 5-2:

A netcat telnet honeypot

Let's start with the simplest form of this honeypot by using this command:

```
sudo ncat -lkp 23
```

Three command-line arguments produce the behavior we want. They are:

- l: Places netcat into "listen-mode" so that it will accept network connections
- k: Forces netcat to allow multiple connections
- p: <port number>: Defines the port netcat listens on

With that command, the listening service starts, and an attacker can connect to the honeypot remotely using a standard telnet client (Figure 5-3). Anything they type prints in the terminal where netcat is running, and conversely, anything typed in that terminal prints to the attacker. Keep in mind that even though the honeypot is running on the telnet port and the attacker connected using the telnet client, netcat accepts any input over the network. So, the attacker could connect with something other than a telnet client, which might show up differently in the connection logs. In the example shown in Figure 5-3, the unrenderable content showing up as question marks is telnet negotiation data sent from the telnet client to the honeypot.

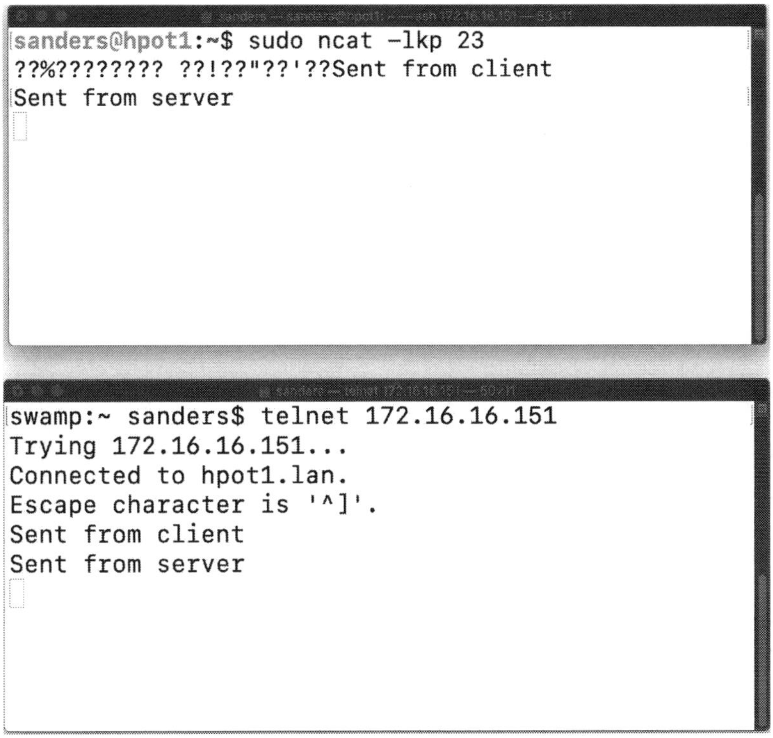

FIGURE 5-3:

The honeypot (top) receives a connection from the attacker (bottom)

The honeypot is also discoverable on the network. Figure 5-4 shows a scan of the system using the Nmap port scanning tool[2]. Port 22 is open for SSH, which I'm using to manage the system the honey service runs on. Port 23 is the honey service I've just created.

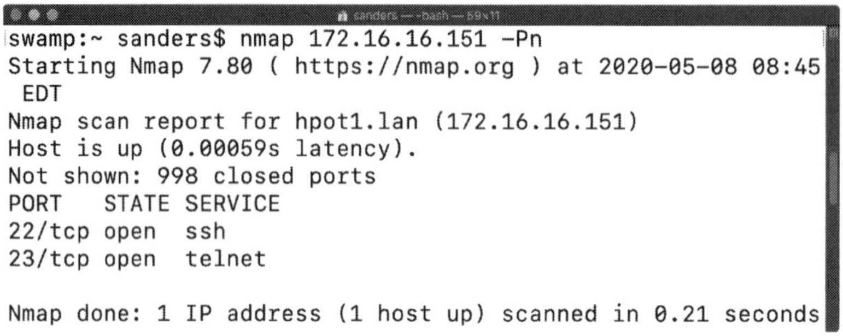

```
swamp:~ sanders$ nmap 172.16.16.151 -Pn
Starting Nmap 7.80 ( https://nmap.org ) at 2020-05-08 08:45
 EDT
Nmap scan report for hpot1.lan (172.16.16.151)
Host is up (0.00059s latency).
Not shown: 998 closed ports
PORT    STATE SERVICE
22/tcp open  ssh
23/tcp open  telnet

Nmap done: 1 IP address (1 host up) scanned in 0.21 seconds
```

FIGURE 5-4:

Running a port scan against the telnet honey service

The honeypot is discoverable, deceptive, and it provides a meaningful interaction. However, it's not monitored. Let's fix that by altering the command to look like this:

```
sudo ncat -klvp 23 >> hpot.log 2>&1
```

The –v argument increases the verbosity of netcat's output, which forces the listener to output the IP address of any system establishing a connection. Netcat logs this information to the console by default, so I use redirection to append the output to a file called hpot.log. Because netcat sends messages out on stderr, a shell trick (2>&1) redirects stderr messages to the same file. Figure 5-5 shows an example of the data logged during a connection. In this example, the attacker connects from 172.16.16.212.

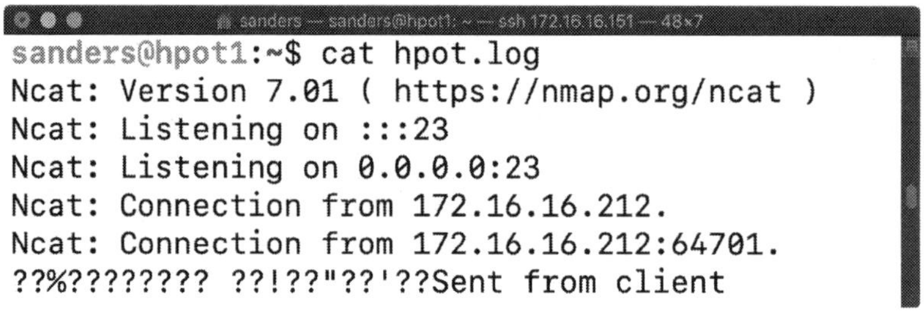

```
sanders@hpot1:~$ cat hpot.log
Ncat: Version 7.01 ( https://nmap.org/ncat )
Ncat: Listening on :::23
Ncat: Listening on 0.0.0.0:23
Ncat: Connection from 172.16.16.212.
Ncat: Connection from 172.16.16.212:64701.
??%???????? ??!??"??'??Sent from client
```

FIGURE 5-5:

Logging honeypot connection attempts

With this basic logging in place, you can monitor the hpot.log file for new connection attempts. Anytime someone connects to the honeypot, it's an alertable event and you'll

---

[2] Learn more about network scanning with Nmap at https://nmap.org/docs.html.

have the source IP address of the connection to begin your investigation.

An HTTP Netcat Honeypot

The telnet honeypot was as simple as it gets, so let's try to expand it using a different example that requires a bit more effort to produce the level of deception, interaction, and monitoring needed.

The goal of this honeypot is to convince an attacker to interact with a fake web server I'll create. There are three requirements this honeypot must meet:

1. It must allow an attacker to browse to a website.
2. It must mimic a legitimate HTTP 403 error page.
3. It must provide robust logging of the HTTP request made to the server along with the source IP address.

We'll still use netcat to achieve these goals, but this requires a bit more logic than we can fit into a single one-line command, so we'll create a bash script[3]. Don't worry if you've never done any scripting; I'll walk you through the example step-by-step. Figure 5-6 shows the entire script.

```
1   PORT=80
2   LOG=hpot.log
3   BANNER=`cat index.html`
4
5   touch /tmp/hpot.hld
6   echo "" >> $LOG
7
8   while [ -f /tmp/hpot.hld ]
9   do
10    echo "$BANNER" | ncat -lvnp $PORT 1>> $LOG 2>> $LOG
11    echo "==ATTEMPTED CONNECTION TO PORT $PORT AT `date`==" >> $LOG
12    echo "" >> $LOG
13    echo "~~~~~~~~~~~~~~~~~~~~~~~~~~~~~~~~~~~~~~~~~~~~~~~~~~~~~" >> $LOG
14  done
```

FIGURE 5-6:

The netcat HTTP honeypot script

Lines 2-4 of the HTTP honeypot script define the variables that dictate how the honeypot works. Using variables for these options allows us to configure the behavior of the honeypot without having to edit multiple references to them in the code. The

---

[3] Now seems like a good time to remind you that all code samples from this book are available online at https://github.com/chrissanders/idh.

variables are:

- PORT: The port the honeypot listens on. I've chosen the default HTTP port 80.
- LOG: The log file storing the honeypot output. The script creates this log file in the directory the honeypot is executed from unless otherwise specified here.
- BANNER: The data displayed to the attacker when they browse to the honeypot webpage. I've referenced an HTML file that contains the HTTP 403 error page shown in Figure 5-7.

Lines 6 and 7 create a temporary lock file (/tmp/hpot.hld) to ensure that only one instance of the honeypot is running at a given time. It also creates the *hpot.log* file if one doesn't already exist.

Lines 9 through 15 are where most of the magic happens. It breaks down like this:

- Line 9 and 10: A WHILE loop initiates the honeypot and keeps it running
- Line 11: The HTML file specified in the $BANNER variable is piped to netcat
- Line 12-14: The script redirects the netcat output to the log file. The output includes the request data sent from the connected client, the client's IP address, a line including the date of the connection, and a separator to divide unique log entries.

```
1  <!DOCTYPE HTML PUBLIC "-//IETF//DTD HTML 2.0//EN">
2  <html><head>
3  <title>403 Forbidden</title>
4  </head><body>
5  <h1>Forbidden</h1>
6  <p>You don't have permission to access URL on this server.</p>
7  <hr>
8  <p><i>Apache/2.4.18 (Ubuntu) Server at 172.16.16.151 Port 80</i></p>
9  </body></html>
```

FIGURE 5-7:

The HTTP 403 Forbidden page sent to attackers who connect to the honeypot

To run the script, execute it directly in the terminal.

```
sudo ./ncpot_http.sh
```

An attacker attempting a connection to the honeypot using a web browser will see the rendered contents of index.html, which looks like a standard HTTP 403 Forbidden page

(Figure 5-8)[4].

FIGURE 5-8:

The attacker sees this page when they browse to the honeypot

It's important to note that while the data provided by the honeypot is transmitted with the HTTP protocol, analysis of the network traffic will reveal abnormalities that are artifacts of the approach. In this case, even though the web page served by the honeypot indicates an HTTP 403 Forbidden response, the HTTP headers will show an HTTP 200 Ok response. This isn't a game breaker since the interaction will have already occurred, but it could mean the attacker eventually figures out something weird is going on if they start digging deeper.

On your end, you'll receive a detailed log of the attacker's connection. In addition to the source IP address, you'll also get the details of the HTTP request, as shown in Figure 5-9. This data provides valuable information about the source, including the user agent, which indicates the tool the attacker used to make the request. You'll use this to determine if the request came from a legitimate browser, an unexpected third-party browser, or something automated like a scanning and enumeration script.

---

[4] You'll see that the IP address of the honeypot is hard coded into the HTML page. You'll adjust this for your own system, or consider adding logic into the script to do this for you.

```
Ncat: Version 7.01 ( https://nmap.org/ncat )
Ncat: Listening on :::80
Ncat: Listening on 0.0.0.0:80
Ncat: Connection from 172.16.16.212.
Ncat: Connection from 172.16.16.212:65053.
GET / HTTP/1.1
Host: 172.16.16.151
Connection: keep-alive
Cache-Control: max-age=0
DNT: 1
Upgrade-Insecure-Requests: 1
User-Agent: Mozilla/5.0 (Macintosh; Intel Mac OS X 10_15_4) AppleWe
bKit/537.36 (KHTML, like Gecko) Chrome/79.0.3945.130 Safari/537.36
Accept: text/html,application/xhtml+xml,application/xml;q=0.9,image
/webp,image/apng,*/*;q=0.8,application/signed-exchange;v=b3;q=0.9
Accept-Encoding: gzip, deflate
Accept-Language: en-US,en;q=0.9

==ATTEMPTED CONNECTION TO PORT 80 AT Fri May  8 09:21:02 EDT 2020==

~~~~~~~~~~~~~~~~~~~~~~~~~~~~~~~~~~~~~~~~~~~~~~~~~~~~~~~~~~~~~~
```

FIGURE 5-9:

The netcat HTTP honeypot log provides information about the attacker's browser

I chose to use an HTTP 403 Forbidden page because it provides another opportunity to control what the attacker thinks and does by carefully selecting what they see. The 403 page indicates that the web server is active and is hosting content, but that the URL needed to access that content isn't readily apparent. Most attackers will see this as a challenge and start probing the server by entering several common URLs in an attempt to find one that is accessible. This technique provides an opportunity to reveal information that can help you determine the attacker's focus. For example, the honeypot log output in Figure 5-10 indicates the attacker might be looking for an authentication page they can attempt to authenticate to.

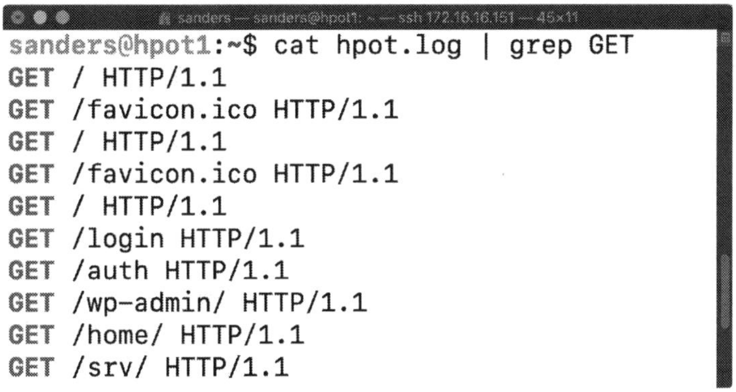

```
● ● ●          sanders — sanders@hpot1: ~ — ssh 172.16.16.151 — 45×11
sanders@hpot1:~$ cat hpot.log | grep GET
GET / HTTP/1.1
GET /favicon.ico HTTP/1.1
GET / HTTP/1.1
GET /favicon.ico HTTP/1.1
GET / HTTP/1.1
GET /login HTTP/1.1
GET /auth HTTP/1.1
GET /wp-admin/ HTTP/1.1
GET /home/ HTTP/1.1
GET /srv/ HTTP/1.1
```

FIGURE 5-10:

The attacker interacting with this honeypot is looking for an authentication page

This HTTP honeypot is more complicated than the telnet honeypot but provides more useful information to help begin an investigation.

> ## *FROM THE TRENCHES:*
>
> As a network defender, few things make me happier than hearing about thwarted attempts to breach networks. One network penetration tester told me that he had gotten caught by honeypots twice in the last year. On one occasion, an SMB honeypot caught him enumerating a fake network share. In another, he was pillaging a user's mailbox and found a URL that looked to be associated with a development instance of the software the company produced. He visited the URL, only to find out later that it was a honeypot set up for the sole purpose of detecting when the user's mailbox had been compromised. That web server he connected to was built using netcat, similarly to what I've shown you here.

Conclusion

This is the first chapter where you've had an opportunity to bring the theory we've discussed earlier in the book to practice. I've shown you how to create two simple service honeypots using netcat. These examples are flexible and well suited to deployment on network segments where any connection to the honeypot is suspicious. Like many other examples you'll read about later, these honeypots don't require expensive hardware or significant financial investment. They could easily be configured to run on a Raspberry Pi or similar microcomputer platforms as purpose-built honeypot devices.

While it will be great if you can take these examples and build onto them or use them on your network, the real goal of this chapter was to demonstrate just how simple honeypots can be. A honeypot doesn't require a massive investment in sophisticated software. Realistically, the best honeypots are often the simplest. In the next several chapters, I'll demonstrate more examples of simple honeypots you can deploy effectively on your network.

HONEY SERVICES 6

YOU CAN MIMIC MANY OF THE LEGITIMATE SERVICES
used on your network as honeypots. In this chapter, I'll walk you
through creating a few service honeypots utilizing a variety of tools
and techniques. I'll start by demonstrating dedicated RDP and SSH
service-specific honeypots before approaching more complex multi-
service honeypots. In each section, I'll provide a breakdown of how
the honeypot can best be deceptive, discoverable, interactive, and
monitored.

Because these honeypots will exist in the complex ecosystem of your own network, I
can't provide a complete step-by-step process from deployment to monitoring. However,
I hope that an overview of the approach and common pitfalls will help you get started
toward deploying your honeypots.

A Windows RDP Honeypot

Microsoft Remote Desktop Protocol (RDP) allows interactive graphical access to
servers and workstations. Systems administrators frequently leverage RDP for remote
troubleshooting and maintenance, while users rely on the service to access interactive
applications without physical access to a system (Figure 6-1).

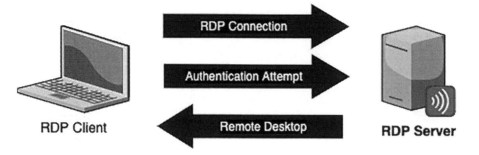

FIGURE 6-1:

Remote Desktop Protocol allows for convenient interactive graphical access

The same reasons that make RDP appealing for legitimate use also make it enticing for attackers seeking to further their influence on a compromised network. At a minimum, attackers often connect to RDP-enabled systems to profile the underlying operating system and will sometimes attempt to guess passwords of known usernames. In many cases, they make a note of these systems to revisit later. Attackers who succeed in obtaining legitimate credentials frequently test those credentials against previously discovered RDP services to further their access. Achieving access to a graphical interface allows for greater (and often more effortless) interactivity for human attackers. These scenarios all present an opportunity to detect attackers connecting to RDP honey services.

 SEE: The goal is for the attacker to see a Windows system inside the network listening on a standard RDP port and providing RDP services.

 THINK: The attacker should think the server is a legitimate business asset running RDP for administrator or user interactivity on the system.

 DO: When the user connects to the service using an RDP client, we'll know they are on the network.

Configuring the Honeypot

In most cases, you should already be familiar with how a service functions before creating a honeypot based on it. Since you'll already know how to set up and configure the service, sometimes it makes sense to simply use a locked down version of that service for your honeypot rather than emulating the service with other software. That's what we'll do here for RDP, leveraging the built-in remote desktop functionality of a Windows system.

Complete these steps to enable remote desktop on Windows 10[1]:

1. Click on the **Start Menu** and choose the **Settings** icon.
2. Choose the **System** option and select **Remote Desktop** from the menu on the left.
3. Click the **Enable Remote Desktop** slider so that it is in the **On** position.
4. Enable the option to **Keep my PC awake for connections when it is plugged in**.

You can learn more about different configuration options for remote desktop on Windows 10 from Microsoft here: https://docs.microsoft.com/en-us/windows-server/remote/remote-desktop-services/clients/remote-desktop-allow-access.

Discoverability

Before deploying the honeypot, you should consider where you'll place it for maximum discoverability given the needs of your network. Because RDP is a network service, attackers already in the network are most likely to discover it through network scanning. This discovery method emphasizes network placement.

Because remote desktop comes with inherent dangers in stolen credential or lateral movement scenarios, network administrators are sometimes reluctant to enable RDP across sensitive assets or near common footholds. Therefore, open RDP ports are inherently unique, dictating the stand-out placement strategy. Placing the RDP honeypot next to common footholds (outside-in strategy) is more likely to catch attackers early, but will be more prone to false positives from accidental connections. Placing the RDP honeypot next to valuable network assets (inside-out strategy) is likely to catch attackers during the later stages of their attacks but will experience fewer false positives. In either case, plan to use the default RDP port (3389) for hosting this service to ensure the attacker's scans pick it up and that they recognize it.

Beyond network scanning, there is more you can do to help attackers discover your RDP honeypot. Creating remote desktop shortcut icons is one of my favorite breadcrumb techniques. These icons are hard-coded links to an IP address or DNS name of the remote desktop server that users can double-click to connect immediately. To create an RDP icon, do this:

1. Right click anywhere on the desktop or in a blank folder space in

---

[1] You can perform these steps on a standalone system or a domain member, but this service is only available on Windows 10 Pro and Enterprise editions.

Windows Explorer. Hover over **New** and click **Shortcut.**

2. In the textbox, type **mstsc /v:HoneypotName**. Replace **HoneypotName** with the DNS name or IP address of the honeypot system (Figure 6-2). Click **Next**.

3. Type a name for the shortcut. The name should be descriptive enough to be enticing, leveraging whatever decoy name you've given the honeypot system. Click **Finish**.

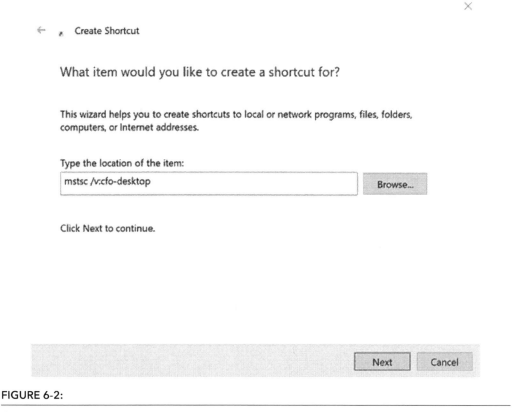

FIGURE 6-2:

Creating an RDP Icon

You can copy and paste these icons into shared folders, mapped drives, or file system root directories. Just remember that the more visible these icons are to real users, the more likely they are to double-click them and trip false alarms. Now that attackers can find the RDP honeypot, we need to give them something to do.

Interactivity

When an attacker connects to the RDP service, the system presents them with the opportunity to supply credentials and log in. If the credentials are valid, they authenticate and gain access to the interactive desktop. If not, they get an error message and can try again or disconnect. These distinct events provide different levels of information that will aid the investigation.

For most organizations, you'll be best served by not allowing anyone to authenticate to the RDP-enabled system successfully. Any connection at all is suspicious, and through Windows event logging, even failed logins provide useful information like the username attempting the authentication and the source host of the attempt. This information provides plenty of fodder for launching an investigation into the source of the potential compromise.

You can limit the attacker's ability to successfully authenticate to the system by limiting the users who have permission to authenticate remotely. By default, members of the local administrators group can log in through remote desktop services. You can limit this ability by editing the local security policy of the honeypot with these steps:

1. Click in the Windows search bar, type **secpol.msc**, and press **Enter**.
2. Browse to **Local Policies/User Rights Assignment** and double click **Deny log on through Remote Desktop Services**.
3. Click **Add User or Group.**
4. Type the name of a user in the Administrators group (Administrator is probably a good place to start) and press **Enter**. Repeat this process for all members of the Administrators group.
5. Click **OK** to apply the policy.

If you add every administrative user to this policy list, you have effectively exposed the RDP service while not allowing anyone to use it successfully. That would be a problem for production systems, but it's perfect for this honeypot. Now that we've given the attacker something to do, we need to watch them.

Monitoring

RDP honeypots provide an opportunity for monitoring at the network and host level (Figure 6-3), although the most value will come from host logs generated by the Windows operating system.

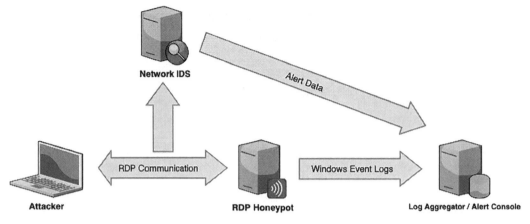

FIGURE 6-3:

RDP Honeypot Monitoring

Using the minimal level of interactivity I've specified, a Windows 10 system generates a couple of interesting logs:

Event ID: 1149

Provider: Microsoft/Windows/TerminalServices-RemoteConnectionManager/Operational

Event Description: User authentication succeeded

Behavior: This event indicates someone successfully authenticated to the system using the RDP service[2].

Enablement: This log is enabled by default.

Investigative Details:

- **Logged/Timestamp**: When the attacker authenticated. Use this to plot a point on your investigation timeline.
- **Source IP**: Where the connection is sourced from on the network. This could be a potentially compromised system.
- **Username**: The username from the client software, if provided. This could be a compromised account.

Event ID: 4625

Provider: Microsoft-Windows-Security-Auditing

Description: An account failed to log on

---

[2] The behavior of this event changed starting with Windows 7 and Server 2008. This blog post explains more about this behavior and how the event functioned previously: https://dfironthe-mountain.wordpress.com/2019/02/15/rdp-event-log-dfir/.

Behavior: This event reports failed attempts to authenticate to a system, regardless of the logon type or whether the account is disabled.

Enablement: For this log to be generated, the *Audit logon events* policy must be enabled in the local security policy and configured to audit failures[3].

Investigative Details:

- **Logged/Timestamp**: When the attacker attempted authentication. Use this to plot a point on your investigation timeline.
- **Network Information/Workstation Name** [WorkstationName]: The system where the logon occurred from.
- **Network Information/Source Network Address** [IpAddress]: The network location where the logon occurred from, if applicable. This could be a compromised system.
- **Subject/Account** [SubjectUserName]: The name of the account reporting the logon failure. This could be a compromised account.
- **Failure Reason** [FailureReason]: The reason the user wasn't allowed to authenticate. There are two primary things you'll see here. The reason "Unknown user name or bad password" indicates the attacker failed authentication because the username and password combination weren't valid. The reason "The user has not been granted the requested logon type at this machine" indicates the username and password were correct, but the login was denied by the permission restrictions you set on the system. This differentiation helps you determine if the potential attacker possesses stolen credentials from a compromised account.

You can generate alerts whenever these events are encountered on RDP honeypot systems because nobody should ever connect to them or attempt to authenticate. EID 1149 indicates successful authentication[4], and EID 4625 indicates failed authentication. The latter should be the most common since this honeypot isn't configured to allow any users. But, it's useful to monitor the former in case of a misconfiguration. I've provided Sigma[5] rules below that you can convert into any number of detection signature formats.

---

[3] This page describes that policy setting and how to enable it: https://docs.microsoft.com/en-us/windows/security/threat-protection/auditing/basic-audit-logon-events.

[4] You can also monitor EID 4624. This event logs successful authentication and is the compliment to EID 4625. It provides similar investigative details.

[5] Sigma is an open and generic signature format for SIEM rules. You can learn more about Sigma at https://github.com/Neo23x0/sigma.

In both examples, the signature filters out known network scanning tools like port and vulnerability scanning applications. Alternatively, you could exclude the honeypots from the scanners.

```
title: Successful Login to RDP Honeypot
description: Connection to RDP honeypot system
date: 2020/01/01
tags:
    - honeypot
author: Chris Sanders
logsource:
    product: windows
    service: Terminal Services
detection:
    selection:
        EventID: 1149
        Computer: %HONEYPOT_NAME_HERE%
    filter:
        "Source Network Address": %CREDENTIALED_SCANNERS%
    condition: selection and not filter
fields:
- "Source Network Address"
- "User"
falsepositives:
    - Undocumented Credentialed Scanners
    - User Errors
level: high
```

```
title: Failed RDP Login Attempt to Honeypot
description: Attempted RDP login to honeypot system
date: 2020/01/01
tags:
    - honeypot
author: Chris Sanders
logsource:
    product: windows
    service: security
detection:
    selection:
        EventID: 4625
        Computer: %HONEYPOT_NAME_HERE%
    filter:
        "Source Network Address": %SCANNERS%
    condition: selection and not filter
fields:
- "Source Network Address"
- "Account Name"
```

```
falsepositives:
    - Undocumented Scanners
    - User Errors
level: high
```

From a network detection perspective, you'll only have visibility into RDP connectivity if the attacker crosses a sensor boundary to connect with the honeypot. This will limit organizations that only place IDS sensors at the network edge. Even if the attacker's connection crosses the sensor boundary, you'll be limited because remote desktop sessions are encrypted. You can still detect connections to the listening RDP port on the honeypot using a simple network detection signature. I've provided a Suricata[6] signature below that will help here:

```
alert tcp !$rdp_honeypot_exclusions any -> honeypot_IP_here 3389
(msg:"RDP Honeypot Connection Attempt"; flow:to_server,established;
threshold: type limit, track by_src, count 100, seconds 600;
classtype:honeypot; sid:50000001; rev:1;)
```

This signature alerts on any connection attempt to the honeypot IP on port 3389 as long as it does not come from a list of exclusions (**!$rdp_honeypot_exclusions**) that likely contains documented network scanning tools. That exclusion list should contain IP addresses of legitimate systems on your network that might communicate with the honeypot such as network scanners, update servers, antivirus consoles, and management servers. The signature only alerts on established network connections (**flow:to_server,established**), so you'll reduce false positives at the expense of missing simple TCP SYN scans. Some additional thresholding[7] limits the number of alerts received for multiple connections from the same source in a short period.

You should customize both the Sigma and Suricata signatures to best fit the needs of your network and specific implementation.

Going Farther

You can extend the RDP honeypot by increasing its interactivity so that you might learn more about potential attackers. With authenticated RDP access, you can observe the attacker downloading additional tools, targeting other systems, or embedding persistence mechanisms that they might use elsewhere.

---

[6] Suricata is a leading free and open source network detection engine. You can learn more about Suricata at https://suricata-ids.org/.

[7] Learn more about Suricata rule thresholding at https://suricata.readthedocs.io/en/suricata-5.0.2/rules/thresholding.html.

Allowing logins to the system creates the most significant interactivity gain, but also adds a great deal of complexity and danger. This decision requires that you enable maximum logging, use network controls to limit who the honeypot can communicate with, actively monitor connections 24/7/365, and have a quick kill switch to terminate the machine in case an attacker starts doing something particularly nefarious. Overall, enabling this level of interactivity is an enormous undertaking and something I generally recommend against for most organizations.

FROM THE TRENCHES:

An incident responder once told me how they used honeypots to assist in an ongoing investigation. The responder's team was called into action by an organization who knew an attacker compromised their network because some sensitive data from the company wound up being published for sale on a cybercrime forum. The organization had very little logging and monitoring infrastructure, so they had no ability to quickly determine the extent of the compromise. However, by monitoring the forum where the sensitive data was for sale, they knew that the attackers had persistent access and were actively marketing newly stolen data frequently. The organization was highly segmented and globally distributed, so the responder's team rapidly deployed service honeypots across multiple network segments. In just a couple of days, the attackers located and attempted to interact with the service honeypots. The response team now had a partial sense of which network segments the attackers had compromised and could focus their efforts in these areas.

SSH Honeypot with Cowrie

Secure Shell (SSH) is the de facto standard for connecting to a remote system using a terminal. The SSH network protocol creates an encrypted tunnel, and the SSH client and server applications provide an authentication mechanism and interactivity between the end user's terminal window and the server's file system (Figure 6-4).

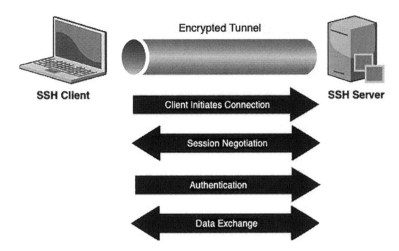

FIGURE 6-4:

A simplified SSH communication sequence

Most administrators manage Linux, Unix, and BSD infrastructure remotely with SSH. Aside from traditional servers, managed devices also include embedded systems like those found in routers, switches, access points, and other networking hardware. The prevalence of SSH, along with the likelihood of attackers targeting devices running it makes it a fantastic candidate for honeypot mimicry.

 SEE: The goal is for the attacker to see a Linux system inside the network listening on a common SSH port and providing SSH services.

 THINK: The attacker should think the server is a legitimate business asset running SSH for system administration.

 DO: When someone connects to the service using an SSH client, we'll know they are on the network. When they interact with the underlying (fake) file system, we'll learn more about their goals and tactics.

Configuring the Honeypot

Instead of using a legitimate SSH server, we'll facilitate this deception with Cowrie, an SSH honeypot developed by Michel Oosterhof. Cowrie is based on another SSH honeypot called Kippo but was forked to its own project in 2015. Cowrie provides a robust feature set that includes:

- An authentication mechanism.
- A post-authentication shell environment.

- A fake file system with the ability to add your own files.
- Several flexible logging and output modes.
- Additional support for Telnet.

You can read more about Cowrie and find installation instructions at: https://github.com/micheloosterhof/cowrie.

The default configuration file at **cowrie/etc/cowrie.cfg.dist** controls how Cowrie executes and runs, providing a standard configuration that will create a honeypot with default attributes listening on port TCP/2222, emulating an x86-64 Linux system. Start Cowrie with the command:

```
bin/cowrie start
```

Using this default, attackers can discover the honeypot with simple port scans, connect to it using a standard SSH client, and authenticate and interact with a fake file system, as I demonstrate below.

```
swamp:~ sanders$ sudo nmap -sV 172.16.16.195 -Pn
Starting Nmap 7.80 ( https://nmap.org ) at 2019-12-06 10:05 EST
Nmap scan report for idh.lan (172.16.16.195)
Host is up (0.00071s latency).
Not shown: 998 closed ports
PORT     STATE SERVICE
22/tcp   open  ssh     OpenSSH 7.6p1 Ubuntu 4ubuntu0.3 (Ubuntu Linux;
protocol 2.0)
2222/tcp open  ssh     OpenSSH 6.0p1 Debian 4+deb7u2 (protocol 2.0)
Service Info: OS: Linux; CPE: cpe:/o:linux:linux_kernel

Service detection performed. Please report any incorrect results at
https://nmap.org/submit/ .
Nmap done: 1 IP address (1 host up) scanned in 6.47 seconds

swamp:~ sanders$ ssh root@172.16.16.195 -p2222
root@172.16.16.195's password:
root@svr04:~# ls /
bin          boot          cdrom         dev
etc          home          initrd.img    initrd.img.old
lib          lib64         lost+found    media
mnt          opt           proc          root
run          sbin          snap          srv
swap.img     sys           tmp           usr
var          vmlinuz       vmlinuz.old
```

In this example, I use the popular port scanning utility Nmap to perform a TCP service probe scan (**-sV**) against the honeypot (**172.16.16.195**). I've also specified that this should be a pingless scan (**-Pn**) since the honeypot isn't configured to respond to pings. The honeypot responds reporting that port 22/tcp is open (the legitimate locked down SSH service), as is port 2222/tcp (the honeypot SSH service run by Cowrie). After this, I connect to the honey service on 172.16.16.195:2222 using the built-in SSH client. Once authenticated using the root username and any password, I list the contents of the file system (**ls /**).

You'll want to make changes to the standard Cowrie configuration to get the most out of it. To make configuration changes, you might be tempted to edit the default cowrie.cfg. dist file, and that will work temporarily, but updates to Cowrie overwrite any change to that file. Instead, you should create a new file named cowrie.cfg and place configuration settings there. Cowrie gives preference to this file if it exists. To make this easier, copy cowrie.cfg.dist to cowrie.cfg and customize the configuration from there.

Discoverability

SSH is ubiquitous on modern networks since it's the most common way to manage Unix-based devices. If your sensitive assets are servers running SSH, then you may choose to mirror them and place SSH honeypots in contiguous IP space using similar ports. Alternatively, you can position individual SSH honeypots to appear unique, perhaps using alternative ports that are still commonly associated with SSH (like 2222/tcp).

Cowrie runs on port TCP/2222 by default, but you might want to change that to fit your chosen discoverability strategy. Configure Cowrie to use the SSH port of your choosing by changing the port number in the **listen_endpoints** variable in the Cowrie configuration file and issuing the **cowrie/bin/cowrie restart** command to restart the service.

If you plan to use SSH to manage the host running the SSH honeypot, you'll need to consider what port that service listens on as well. You'll effectively have two ports open on the system; one for the legitimate SSH service and one for the honeypot service. If you want to stand out, a system running SSH on two different ports would undoubtedly do that. But, both services can't exist on the same port. Work around this limitation by configuring the system firewall to limit inbound connections to the legitimate SSH port from a specified range of IP addresses, most likely belonging to the IT and security teams.

This command configures a system running the ufw firewall (which ships disabled on Ubuntu Linux, but denies incoming connections by default when turned on) only to allow connections to port 2222 from the 192.168.12.0/24 range:

If you'd like to add in another layer of obfuscation to your additional SSH port, consider port knocking. Like a rhythmic knocking sequence on a dark alley door grants entrance into a prohibition-era speakeasy, port knocking grants access to services on a host when a prospective client transmits the right course of packets (Figure 6-5).

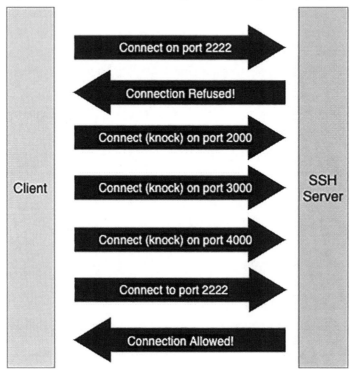

FIGURE 6-5:

Port Knocking to Access Hidden SSH

Port knocking works by configuring the local firewall of a system to block all inbound communication to a port hosting a legitimate service (like SSH). At the same time, the port knocking service opens up several additional ports and listens for connections. When a client connects to those ports in the correct sequence, the server adds the client's IP address to the firewall's allow-list for the legitimate service port. No other client readily knows the port is open or can connect to it without the unique connection sequence. While this technique isn't foolproof, the extra layer of obscurity helps further the honeypot deception while allowing access to services needed to maintain those systems.

For a step-by-step guide to configuring port knocking using knockd on Ubuntu, see here: https://help.ubuntu.com/community/PortKnocking.

Attackers are most likely to discover SSH honey services from network scanning, but there's one trick I like to use to lure them into my honeypots from other compromised hosts. This breadcrumb involves seeding the bash history files of other Linux hosts with references to the honeypot. Attackers frequently enumerate bash history files of compromised assets to learn more about the system and find other hosts for potential lateral movement, so it's likely for an attacker to discover our honeypot here.

Fortunately, you don't have to connect to your honeypot from every Linux system to seed the bash history file. Using the **history -s** command will let you add something to history without executing it, as shown below.

```
swamp:~ sanders$ history -s ssh 172.16.16.192
swamp:~ sanders$ history
    1  ifconfig
    2  time
    3  ssh 172.16.16.192
    4  history
```

In the above example, I never created an SSH connection to the honeypot, but an attacker wouldn't quickly know that. Instead, they see that the user on the system they're interacting with initiated an SSH connection to 172.16.16.192. It looks just as real as the **ifconfig** and **time** commands, which I did run. To distribute these breadcrumbs, consider scripting this command to seed entries like this into history files of users across multiple systems periodically. This BASH one-liner adds the SSH connection string to a random spot in the history file for a user. You can pair this script with existing configuration management tools like Chef or Ansible for deployment at scale.

```
sed -i "$((1 + $RANDOM % `cat ~/.bash_history | wc -l`)) a ssh
172.16.16.192" ~/.bash_history
```

In its default configuration, an attacker could easily tip you off to their presence by scanning Cowrie's SSH port or even attempting a connection to it. That's enough to let you know that they're on the network, but you won't get much information about the attacker. To elicit more information, we'll entice attackers to stick around and play more by leveraging further deception and interactivity.

Interactivity

By making attackers believe your honeypot is a legitimate system, you increase the chance that the attacker will provide you with facets of their tradecraft by issuing unique commands, seeking out specific files, or uploading additional tools or malware. You'll also increase their time cost to attack your network the longer they engage with the honeypot, delaying their next action while you're already conducting an investigation. Cowrie provides significant flexibility to deceive attackers, so let's discuss a few things you can do to increase deception and interactivity and get more value from your SSH honeypot.

Changing the Hostname and Banners

Right off the bat, attackers derive information from what the honeypot directly advertises to them. Easily recognizable defaults could tip off an attacker about the honeypot, so you'll want to adjust these low-hanging fruits to further your deception.

To change the server banner (default svr04), change the **hostname** variable in cowrie. cfg to something else. If you're blending in, you'll want to mimic similar server names existing in the network range containing the honeypot. If you want to stand out, pick something unique and unlike other names in the range.

Mimicking login banners that exist on legitimate network systems is helpful here as well. Cowrie shows the pre-login banner when someone connects to the system. You can mirror what you're already using in your organization or customize something generic like what I've done below and place it in **cowrie/honeyfs/etc/issue.net**. You should also consider a post-login banner since many operating systems use one to identify themselves after authentication. To do this, copy the post-login banner from a legitimate system into **cowrie/honeyfs/etc/motd**. An example connection and login sequence with pre and post banners mirroring an Ubuntu 18 server system is shown below.

```
swamp:~ sanders$ ssh root@172.16.16.195 -p2222
* * * * * * * * * * W A R N I N G * * * * * * * * * *
This computer system is the property of Applied Network Defense. It is
for authorized use only. By using this system, all users acknowledge
notice of, and agree to comply with, the organization's Acceptable Use of
Information Technology Resources Policy ("AUP"). Unauthorized or improper
use of this system may result in administrative disciplinary action,
civil charges/criminal penalties, and/or other sanctions as set forth in
the Organization's AUP. By continuing to use this system you indicate
your awareness of and consent to these terms and conditions of use.
If you are physically located in the European Union, you may have
additional rights per the GDPR. Visit the web site dataprivacy.utk.edu
for more information.

LOG OFF IMMEDIATELY if you do not agree to the conditions stated in this
warning.

* * * * * * * * * * * * * * * * * * * * * * * * * * *
root@172.16.16.195's password:
Welcome to Ubuntu 18.04.3 LTS (GNU/Linux 4.15.0-70-generic x86_64)
```

```
 * Documentation:   https://help.ubuntu.com
 * Management:      https://landscape.canonical.com
 * Support:         https://ubuntu.com/advantage
root@svr04:~# id
uid=0(root) gid=0(root) groups=0(root)
```

Manipulating SSH Characteristics

Attackers with heightened awareness may notice default Cowrie SSH protocol features or pick up that they don't match the expected feature set of the operating system you're mimicking. Changing the version of SSH the honeypot advertises helps here. To do this, change the **ssh_version** field in cowrie.cfg. Your best bet is to issue the **ssh -V** command on the system you're mimicking and copy that SSH version string into this variable.

```
sanders@ubuntu:~$ ssh -V
OpenSSH_7.6p1 Ubuntu-4ubuntu0.3, OpenSSL 1.0.2n  7 Dec 2017
```

If you'd like to go a step farther, change the SSH version string, ciphers, and message integrity codes Cowrie presents to the client to achieve consistency with the operating system you're mimicking. Get a list of supported ciphers with **ssh -Q cipher** and message integrity codes with **ssh -Q mac**. These are enabled in the **ciphers** and **macs** variables under the **[ssh]** section in cowrie.cfg. Cowrie doesn't implement every cipher you might find on a legitimate system you're mimicking, so you're limited to the options available in the configuration file and might be unable to create a perfect match.

```
sanders@ubuntu:~$ ssh -Q cipher
3des-cbc
aes128-cbc
aes192-cbc
aes256-cbc
...
sanders@ubuntu:~$ ssh -Q mac
hmac-sha1
hmac-sha1-96
hmac-sha2-256
...
```

Place the SSH version (taken from ssh -V above, the portion before the comma) under the **version** variable, taking care to prepend **SSH-2.0-** at the beginning of the string, as shown in the examples provided in the config file.

You can also derive these SSH characteristics by capturing packets of the initial SSH communication sequence between an SSH client and server and using that information to configure Cowrie as described in this section.

Seeding the Process List

Attackers commonly profile running processes on systems they've just compromised to get a better understanding of what defenses they might be up against or to look for links to interesting data. Cowrie allows listing running processes by emulating the ps command for connected users. But rather than listing the real processes running on the system, it simply dumps a list of process names from a configurable list at **cowrie/share/cowrie/ cmdoutput.json**. Here's an example of process list entry from that file:

```
"command": {
  "ps": [
    {
        "COMMAND": "/usr/sbin/rsyslogd -n",
        "CPU": 0.0,
        "MEM": 0.40309513835647837,
        "PID": 425,
        "RSS": 2088960,
        "START": "Jun22",
        "STAT": "D<",
        "TIME": 0.04,
        "TTY": "?",
        "USER": "root",
        "VSZ": 264880128
    }
```

This entry places the rsyslogd (event logging service) in the ps command output for the honeypot. You get quite a few other configuration options here as well, like the CPU and memory usage, process ID, and the user executing the process.

You could easily spend a lot of time customizing your ps output. Still, once again, I recommend choosing an operating system to emulate and copying a running process list from that system to seed the ps command output. This command simplifies the process by automatically dumping the process list from a system and using jq to format the output appropriately for the cmdoutput.json file:

```
ps -eo pcpu,%mem,pid,rss,start_time,stat,bsdtime,tty,user,vsz,args |
egrep -v '(ps -eo|jq|egrep|awk)' | awk '{for(i=1;i<=10;i++){printf
"%s\t",$i};out=$11; for(i=12;i<=NF;i++){out=out" "$i}; print out}' |
jq -s  --slurp --raw-input --raw-output 'split("\n") | .[1:-1] |
map(split("\t")) | map({"COMMAND": .[10], "CPU": .[0]|tonumber, "MEM":
.[1]|tonumber, "PID": .[2]|tonumber, "RSS": .[3]|tonumber, "START":
.[4], "STAT": .[5], "TIME": .[6], "TTY": .[7], "USER": .[8], "VSZ":
.[9]|tonumber})| { "command": { "ps": .}}'
```

If you want to assess the awareness or skill of the attacker in your honeypot, consider listing a process name tied to a typical antivirus or application allow-listing binary and see if the attacker notices it and tries to kill it.

Seeding User Accounts

When your honeypot emulates a service providing authentication, you get to choose whether you want to allow attackers to pass that authentication process successfully. To do so increases the amount of information you'll get from their post-compromise activity, but also increases the workload for you to maintain believable deception.

For Cowrie, the **cowrie/etc/userdb.txt** file controls authentication and provides instructions for its syntax. If you open this file, you'll see that it's merely a list of user accounts and passwords that can log into the honeypot. It's pretty lax by default. The tomcat and oracle users can log in with any password, indicated by the asterisk (*) in the third column of their respective entries. The root user also appears, but rather than allowing authentication with any password, potential attackers can log in with any password except for a few common entries like 'root' and '123456', indicated by the exclamation point (!).

```
# Example userdb.txt
# This file may be copied to etc/userdb.txt.
# If etc/userdb.txt is not present, built-in defaults will be used.
#
# ':' separated fields, file is processed line for line
# processing will stop on first match
#
# Field #1 contains the username
# Field #2 is currently unused
# Field #3 contains the password
# '*' for password allows any password
# '!' at the start of a password will not grant this password access
# '/' can be used to write a regular expression
#

root:x:!root
root:x:!123456
root:x:!/honeypot/i
root:x:*
tomcat:x:*
oracle:x:*
```

If you only plan to alert on any connection to the honeypot or authentication attempt, then you'll configure this file to disallow any successful authentication by merely removing the entries. However, be careful not to simply delete the file, as Cowrie will revert to these defaults.

If you want to observe the attacker's actions, you'll need to allow them to log in. To enable logins for a specific username, add the new account to the userdb.txt file using the format shown in the above. The easiest way to allow authentication is to use a reasonably generic username with a generic password. For example, admin:x:123 or root:x:password. However, such an easily guessable combination might raise suspicion amongst many attackers and scare them off. A few more practical tips might include:

- Creating easily guessable usernames and passwords tied to your organization name (walmart:x:walmart)
- Leaving credentials lying around on public file shares likely to be accessed in a compromise.
- Utilizing default credentials from common services or devices (cisco:x:cisco). This works best if you also mimic other characteristics of the device.

The changes made to userdb.txt take effect immediately and don't require restarting Cowrie.

Building a More Legitimate File System

When an attacker logs into the SSH honeypot, Cowrie presents them with what appears to be a functioning file system. They can use the **ls** command to list the contents of directories, the **cd** command to change into them, and even use the **cat** command to read out files. The file system looks and feels real at a basic level, but it's all fake and made possible through a database of directories and associated files served up by Cowrie. They aren't actually interacting with a real file system. Any time a user logs in, Cowrie gives them a copy of this file system to manipulate, which gets deleted after they log off.

While the default file system included with cowrie works for proof of concept, there are a few good reasons to replace it with one of your own creation. First, if you hope to keep an adversary engaged with your honeypot for long, you must give them something interesting to dig through. Second, clever or experienced attackers may easily recognize the vanilla honeypot file system or some of its default attributes. Finally, several of the other changes you'll likely make to Cowrie should also be reflected in the file system. For example, if you added users to the userdb.txt file, the file system should contain home directories for those users along with entries in /etc/passwd, /etc/shadow, /etc/group, and other related files.

There are two essential components to the Cowrie emulated filesystem. First is the pickle file[8] that contains a database of the file system metadata like the directory structure, file names, permissions, ownership, and so on. Next is the cowrie/honeyfs directory containing the file contents. For an attacker to find and view a file, it must be present both in the pickle file and in the honeyfs directory structure. If it's in the pickle file but not in honeyfs, they'll find the file, but it won't have any contents. If it's in honeyfs but not in the pickle file, they won't be able to see it in the directory structure.

Creating a pickle file is most effectively done by deploying a reference OS that you'll use as the basis for your fake file system. For example, if you're mirroring an Ubuntu 18 system, deploy a copy of Ubuntu in a VM and configure that file system as you'd want your attacker to view it. From there, complete the following steps:

1. On your honeypot, move the existing honeyfs directory into a backup location:

```
mv honeyfs/ backupfs/
```

2. Copy the entire contents of the remote reference system into the honeyfs directory. One way to do this is with rsync[9], like this (this assumes you have SSH configured on the remote system):

```
rsync -avzhe ssh user@192.168.1.20:/ cowrie/honeyfs/
```

3. Make any changes to the file structure you want reflected in the honeypot system. This might include inserting fake data, modifying the passwd and shadow files to match the user database you created, removing entries from the bash history file, removing anything sensitive if you're mirroring a production system, or other deception-related changes.

4. Use the createfs command to create the pickle file from the honeyfs directory:

```
./bin/createfs -l honeyfs -d 5 -o share/cowrie/ubuntu.pickle
```

- -l: Directory containing the file system to emulate
- -d: Depth of the file system to enumerate
- -o: Output file

5. Modify cowrie.cfg to use the updated pickle file by modifying the **filesystem** variable in the **[shell]** section.

---

[8] Pickle is used by Python to serialize and deserialize objects. I think this is a hilarious name and laugh every time I read it. For the record, bread and butter pickles are the best pickles.

[9] Learn more about rsync and the options I used here: https://linux.die.net/man/1/rsync.

```
filesystem = ${honeypot:share_path}/ubuntu.pickle
```

6. Restart Cowrie.

Now, attackers will see an Ubuntu file system when they authenticate to the honeypot. Any changes to the directory structure or file metadata that you wish for the file system to reflect require creating a new pickle file using createfs. Make changes to file contents by editing them directly in cowrie/honeyfs. If there's a file you want to appear in a directory listing but not output its content, simply remove it from the honeyfs directory structure.

Monitoring

Because Cowrie is a purpose-built honeypot, it provides tremendous flexibility in logging interaction in a variety of output formats. It has a native ability to log directly to Elasticsearch, Syslog, MySQL, MongoDB, Splunk, and other tools[10]. It also records output in a variety of text formats like the default JSON and plaintext formats in cowrie/var/log/cowrie. Because Cowrie generates its logs directly, it usually sends them straight to a log aggregator (Figure 6-6).

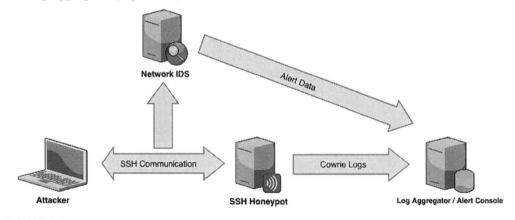

FIGURE 6-6:

Cowrie SSH Honeypot Monitoring

For alerting, what you'll care about depends on the level of interactivity allowed. If you're not allowing successful logins, alert on new connections like shown here:

```
2020-06-22T17:38:23.947119Z cb383b60826d New connection:
172.16.16.212:62703 (172.16.16.195:2222) [session: cb383b60826d]
```

Here's the same log in JSON format, which is less pleasing to the human eye, but

---

[10] See the examples in cowrie.cfg or the official Cowrie documentation to configure these output options.

reveals field names useful for building detection rules:

```
{"eventid":"cowrie.session.connect","src_ip":"172.16.16.212","src_
port":62703,"dst_ip":"172.16.16.195","dst_
port":2222,"session":"cb383b60826d","protocol":"ssh","message":"New
connection: 172.16.16.212:62703 (172.16.16.195:2222) [session: cb383b6082
6d]","sensor":"idh","timestamp":"2020-06-22T17:38:23.947119Z"}
```

This log entry provides the source IP address of the connection to investigate. Here's a Sigma rule for this event based on field names from the JSON version of that same log entry:

```
title: Connection to SSH Honeypot
description: Connection to Cowrie SSH honeypot
date: 2020/01/01
tags:
    - honeypot
author: Chris Sanders
logsource:
    product: cowrie
    service: ssh_honeypot
detection:
    selection:
        eventid: cowrie.session.connect
    filter:
        src_ip: %SCANNERS%
    condition: selection and not filter
fields:
    - "src_ip"
falsepositives:
    - Undocumented Scanners
    - User Errors
level: high
```

If you're allowing interactive logins to the honeypot, you'll only alert after successful authentication like this example:

```
2020-06-22T17:38:25.662388Z cb383b60826d login attempt [sanders/gotcha]
succeeded
```

Here's the same log entry in JSON:

```
{"eventid":"cowrie.login.
success","username":"sanders","password":"gotcha","message":"login
```

attempt [sanders/gotcha] succeeded","sensor":"idh","timestamp":"2020-06-22T17:38:25.662388Z","src_ip":"172.16.16.212","session":"cb383b60826d"}

This log entry provides the source IP address, username, and password. Also notice that both the connection and authentication logs share the same session ID. You can use this unique identifier to track actions across individual sessions. With this information, not only can you begin to investigate the system an attacker presumably has control over, you can also examine the account they compromised. Here's a Sigma rule for this event:

```
title: Successful Authentication to SSH Honeypot
description: Successful authentication to Cowrie SSH honeypot
date: 2020/01/01
tags:
    - honeypot
author: Chris Sanders
logsource:
    product: cowrie
    service: ssh_honeypot
detection:
    selection:
        eventid: cowrie.login.success
    filter:
        src_ip: %SCANNERS%
    condition: selection and not filter
fields:
        - "src_ip"
        - "username"
        - "password"
level: critical
```

Cowrie provides other logs you'll want to store to aid with investigating the alerts you generate from it. The most useful are command input logs, which register the terminal commands the attacker used, even if they didn't work. This one shows an attacker listing the contents of the /etc/passwd file.

```
2020-04-09T18:50:03.529277Z [SSHChannel session (0) on SSHService b'ssh-connection' on HoneyPotSSHTransport,5,172.16.16.212] CMD: cat /etc/passwd
```

The event log indicating the attacker's session ended is also important, as it helps you set a time bounding on your analysis window for the honeypot interaction:

```
2020-04-09T18:50:18.800630Z [HoneyPotSSHTransport,5,172.16.16.212]
```

Going Farther

If you continue perusing cowrie.cfg, you'll find that I've only scratched the surface of its capabilities. There's quite a bit more that you can do to increase the interactivity and deception of Cowrie-based SSH honeypots like adjusting default timeouts, adding in support for additional interactive commands, or even proxying cowrie to a real SSH shell rather than an emulated one.

While I'm cautious about allowing extensive interactivity on honeypots built from real services, tools like Cowrie provide an opportunity to go much farther without significant added risk thanks to a smaller attack surface. By leveraging a few of the configuration options identified here along with other discoverability and interactivity best practices discussed throughout this book, you'll end up with a honeypot that provides an abundance of intelligence about your attacker's tools and tactics.

Multi-Service Honeypots with OpenCanary

Every honeypot I've shown you thus far focuses on mimicking a single service. Now, we're going to look at a honeypot designed to emulate multiple services. While multi-service honeypots don't usually offer the configuration granularity of single service honeypots, they make up for it with their breadth of potential and the administrator's ability to only have to manage a single application, configuration syntax, and logging format across honeypot deployments.

OpenCanary is a free, open-source honeypot maintained by Thinkst. Using similar technology to their commercial offering, it provides a simple Python-based platform for deploying different honey services using a simple JSON configuration file.

OpenCanary supports quite a few services: GIT, FTP, HTTP, SMB, MySQL, SSH, SNMP, SIP, VNC, and more. Let's create an HTTP honeypot with OpenCanary. HTTP servers are popular targets for attackers because they often expose a large attack surface, provide a place to utilize previously stolen credentials, and sometimes host poorly maintained applications that are ripe for exploitation.

 SEE: The goal is for the attacker to see a system inside the network listening on a common HTTP port and hosting a web page.

THINK: The attacker should think the server is a legitimate business asset running some form of web page or service.

 DO: When someone makes an HTTP request to the honeypot, we'll know they are on the network. We'll provide an authentication page, so the honeypot entices them to supply credentials they may have harvested.

Configuring the Honeypot

You can download OpenCanary from https://github.com/thinkst/opencanary and install it using the instructions here: https://opencanary.readthedocs.io/en/latest/starting/opencanary.html.

After installation, generate a configuration file by running the following command:

```
opencanaryd --copyconfig
```

The configuration file is at ~/.opencanary.conf in JSON format. You can edit the file using whatever text editor you like, but take care to maintain proper JSON formatting or OpenCanary will fail to start. I like to use jq to validate the JSON after making changes:

1. Install jq

```
sudo apt-get install jq
```

2. Parse the file with jq. If everything's fine, jq shows the properly formatted file contents. If something's wrong, it'll give you an error message along with the line and column of the problem:

```
jq . .opencanary.conf
```

Before enabling any services, you'll want to configure the device.node_id variable in opencanary.conf. The value you place here identifies the honeypot, so assign unique values to every instance of OpenCanary you've got running.

The default configuration contains every available option you have at your disposal, but individual services must be enabled and configured before starting the OpenCanary service.

There are several options available for HTTP honeypot configuration:

```
"http.banner": "Apache/2.2.22 (Ubuntu)",
  "http.enabled": false,
  "http.port": 80,
```

```
"http.skin": "nasLogin",
"http.skindir": ""
```

To start the HTTP service with the default options, just change http.enabled to **true** and start OpenCanary[11]:

```
opencanaryd --start
```

The service is now listening on port 80 and accessible with a web browser (Figure 6-7). Browsing to it reveals a fake Synology NAS Login screen. The service logs any credentials submitted to the form but doesn't permit successful authentication.

FIGURE 6-7:

The Default Web Service Skin

There are a few other options we can play around with here, so let's look at those now in the context of discoverability, interactivity, and monitoring.

Discoverability

Attackers on the network will most likely discover an HTTP honeypot through network scanning. If you're taking a stand-out approach, place the honeypot on a segment with no other web servers, or place it on a segment with other web servers, but change the port the service listens on. To do that, modify the http.port variable in opencanary.conf. Also,

---

[11] The default configuration has the FTP honeypot enabled by default. Be sure to set ftp.enabled to false if you don't want to use that one.

consider changing the HTTP banner setting to something unique in case the attacker's scans are also configured to grab service banners. The default looks like this:

```
"http.banner": "Apache/2.2.22 (Ubuntu)"
```

If you want your honeypot to blend in with similar web services, configure the port and banner variables to match them.

For additional breadcrumbs, consider creating hyperlink icons that point to your honeypot URL and placing them in areas where attackers are likely to find them. Public file shares and file system directory roots are good candidates.

Interactivity

Web application interactivity represents the potential for a sizable attack surface. The default OpenCanary HTTP honeypot provides a simple login screen that entices attackers to attempt the use of harvested credentials, or at the very least, invites credential guessing. However, you probably don't want every HTTP honeypot to look like a Synology NAS. Thankfully, OpenCanary provides a second website option (they refer to these as skins), as well as the flexibility to customize the provided templates or create your own.

You'll find the provided skins under **opencanary/modules/data/http/skin**[12]. The default skin is in the nasLogin folder and a simpler template with a plain login form is under the basicLogin folder. Flex your HTML skills and customize these to your heart's content. Sometimes keeping things ambiguous and simple is most effective, but you can also copy and paste HTML from other legitimate tools to create a more believable veil of deception. Authentication pages for CRM tools, web app management tools, and internal wikis make good candidates for mimicry here.

You can paint this canvas however you see fit, but if you hope to capture authentication usernames from attackers attempting to log in, be sure to preserve the naming of the form input fields. Username should have the name parameter 'username', like the example below.

```
<form method="POST">
        <dl>
        <dt>Username:</dt>
        <dd><input type="text" name="username" /></dd>
```

---

[12] If you're using a Python virtual environment, as recommended in the OpenCanary installation instructions, these will be under env/lib/python2.7/site-packages/opencanary/modules/data/http/skin/. Note that the exact path will depend on your python version, so you'll replace python2.7 here with whatever version you're running.

```
    <dt>Password:</dt>
    <dd><input type="password" name="password" /></dd>
    <dt></dt>
    <dd><input type="submit" value="Login" name="btnLogin" /></dd>
</form>
```

Rather than significantly modifying the existing templates, I prefer to copy them into a new skin. That requires these steps:

1. Copy an existing skin into a new folder[13].

```
cp -r opencanary/modules/data/http/skin/basicLogin/ /home/
sanders/honeysite/wikiLogin
```

2. Modify the contents of index.html or other pages as desired.

3. Edit opencanary.conf. First, provide the location to the skin folder in the http.skindir variable:

```
"http.skindir": "/home/sanders/honeysite/wikiLogin",
```

4. Change the value of the http.skin parameter to a value that you'll recognize. The interaction logging will reflect this value.

```
"http.skin": "wikiLogin"
```

5. Restart OpenCanary

```
opencanaryd --restart
```

Keep in mind that any change to HTTP skins, even just minor HTML changes, requires restarting OpenCanary.

Monitoring

OpenCanary is built on Python, which provides tremendous flexibility in how it writes data. For most of us, however, the default JSON output is flexible enough to ingest into most logging pipelines (Figure 6-8). View or modify the location of this log file under the logger section of opencanary.conf:

```
"file": {
    "class": "logging.FileHandler",
    "filename": "/var/tmp/opencanary.log"
}
```

---

[13] You can also create your HTML from scratch. But, know that OpenCanary requires a 403.html and 404.html error page along with an index page.

The OpenCanary documentation[14] provides examples of other logging options, like transmitting to a Syslog server, sending alert email messages, or even posting Slack messages.

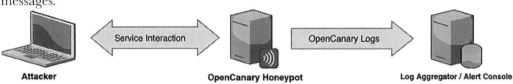

FIGURE 6-8:

OpenCanary honeypot monitoring

The type and verbosity of the log entries depends on the honeypot type. For the HTTP honeypot, you'll be interested in requests for pages, like this:

```
{"dst_host": "172.16.16.195", "dst_port": 80, "local_time": "2020-
04-10 18:57:05.753829", "logdata": {"HOSTNAME": "172.16.16.195",
"PATH": "/index.html", "SKIN": "wikiLogin", "USERAGENT": "Mozilla/5.0
(Macintosh; Intel Mac OS X 10_15_2) AppleWebKit/537.36 (KHTML, like
Gecko) Chrome/79.0.3945.130 Safari/537.36"}, "logtype": 3000, "node_id":
"hpot1", "src_host": "172.16.16.212", "src_port": 61096}
```

This log provides information about the HTTP client, including the source IP address (**172.16.16.212**) and HTTP user agent (**Mozilla/5.0 (Macintosh; Intel Mac OS X 10_15_2) AppleWebKit/537.36 (KHTML, like Gecko) Chrome/79.0.3945.130 Safari/537.36**). With this information, you can begin to investigate the source host with some sense of what level of access the attacker might possess. For example, a browser-based user agent (like the above log entry) indicates some form of interactive access. In contrast, a Nmap or scripting language user agent might indicate that the attacker only has command-line access at this point.

Here's a Sigma rule for this event:

```
title: Connection to HTTP Honeypot
description: Connection to OpenCanary HTTP honeypot
date: 2020/01/01
tags:
    - honeypot
author: Chris Sanders
logsource:
    product: opencanary
    service: http_honeypot
detection:
```

[14] https://opencanary.readthedocs.io/en/latest/starting/configuration.html.

```
    selection:
        logtype: 3000[15]
    filter:
            src_host: %SCANNERS%
    condition: selection and not filter
fields:
    - "src_host"
    - "USERAGENT"
falsepositives:
    - Undocumented Scanners
    - User Errors
level: high
```

For analysts, any interaction with the web server is interesting but multiple visits or significant browsing might generate quite a few alerts for the same activity. In that case, you might only alert on login credential submission, which looks like this:

```
{"dst_host": "172.16.16.195", "dst_port": 80, "local_time": "2020-04-10
19:02:32.253397", "logdata": {"HOSTNAME": "172.16.16.195", "PASSWORD":
"bbq", "PATH": "/index.html", "SKIN": "wikiLogin", "USERAGENT":
"Mozilla/5.0 (Macintosh; Intel Mac OS X 10_15_2) AppleWebKit/537.36
(KHTML, like Gecko) Chrome/79.0.3945.130 Safari/537.36", "USERNAME":
"chris"}, "logtype": 3001, "node_id": "hpot1", "src_host":
"172.16.16.212", "src_port": 61130}
```

Here you see the attacker attempting authentication to the web app with the username 'chris' and the password 'bbq'. This evidence might mean that the attacker previously harvested that user's credentials, which should help direct your investigation.

Here's one more Sigma rule to detect authentication attempts to the HTTP honeypot:

```
title: Authentication Attempt to HTTP Honeypot
description: Someone attempted to authenticate to a login page on an
OpenCanary HTTP honeypot
date: 2020/01/01
tags:
    - honeypot
author: Chris Sanders
logsource:
    product: opencanary
    service: http_honeypot
detection:
    selection:
        logtype: 3001
```

---

[15] Thinkst uses logtype to uniquely identify event types. You'll find a full listing of these events in opencanary/logger.py.

```
    filter:
        src_host: %SCANNERS%
    condition: selection and not filter
fields:
        - "src_host"
        - "USERAGENT"
        - "USERNAME"
        - "PASSWORD"
level: high
```

Going Farther

While multi-service honeypots usually don't provide quite the interactivity or flexibility of real services or emulated single service honeypots, their simplicity means you can stand up honey services quickly. For example, there are only two configuration options required for an RDP honeypot:

```
"rdp.enabled": false
"rdp.port": 3389
```

To set up an RDP honeypot, set rdp.enabled to **true** and start OpenCanary. If you didn't change the rdp.port setting, port 3389 should now be open on the system and responsive to connections from an RDP client. OpenCanary logs any authentication attempts to the system. While there's no ability to allow successful logins and derive attacker tradecraft like in our earlier attempt at creating an RDP honeypot, the simple configuration and reduced attack surface make this method preferable in most cases.

Keep in mind that Thinkst wrote OpenCanary in open source Python. If you've got the skills or want to learn them, you can extend the tool to meet your needs. If you do, just remember to contribute your excellent work back to the project so everyone benefits!

Conclusion

In this chapter, I demonstrated three approaches for deploying honey services. The first used the full Microsoft Remote Desktop service to create an RDP honeypot. The second used an emulated single-service tool called Cowrie to deploy an SSH honeypot. Finally, we looked at a multi-service honeypot tool called OpenCanary to create an HTTP honeypot and explore other services it offered.

It's important to understand that there are tradeoffs between each technique. While real systems might seem ideal because of their interactivity, they require more protection and workarounds to limit the exposed attack surface. Dedicated honeypot applications sometimes require more work to achieve the deception and interactivity you desire. Still, they are often built with monitoring in mind and need less work to make them safe and secure. Considering our mantra that any interaction with a honeypot is interesting and enough to kick off an investigation, you won't often need a high degree of interactivity. For all those reasons, I try to stick with dedicated honeypot applications whenever I can.

HONEY TOKENS 7

IF YOU SPEND ENOUGH TIME IN THE INFOSEC
trenches, you eventually learn that security is much more about the
data than computers. After all, it's the confidentiality, integrity, and
availability of data we're most concerned about and it's the data most
attackers target. If data is most at risk, then it makes sense to apply
deception techniques to protecting that data directly with honey
tokens. Honey tokens are security resources that mimic legitimate data
and are my favorite type of honeypot due to their ease of deployment
and success rate.

In this chapter, I'll demonstrate several ways to use honey tokens to deceive attackers
by mimicking data that probably already exists on your network. We'll look at creating
deceptive Microsoft Office documents, honey files, and honey folders.

Honeydocs

People like to think that most companies' crown jewels exist in complex databases
tied to custom applications segmented from more accessible parts of the network. In
reality, attackers leech the lifeblood from organizations by pillaging office documents—

Excel spreadsheets, PowerPoint presentations, and Word documents (or their non-Microsoft counterparts where applicable). Whether it's a customer list or product design specifications, these documents exist en masse across the personal systems of individual users and on public shared network drives. Attackers will likely have access to some of these places once they compromise different user systems or harvest their credentials. So, let's use this to our advantage!

A *honeydoc* is an Office document containing a honey token for tracking purposes. A common type of honey token used in this application is a web bug. A *web bug* (or web beacon) is an object placed inside a file or folder that references a resource (usually an image) from an external URL[1]. Whenever you open an Office document with a web bug, the application attempts to access the referenced URL. Whoever controls that web server now knows when and where someone opened the document (Figure 7-1). Web bug users typically hide them by shrinking them down to a 1x1 pixel, so it's not easily noticed by whoever opens the document.

FIGURE 7-1:

A web bug in a honeydoc allows you to track when someone opens it

Let's create our own honeydoc now from scratch. We'll implant a web bug in a Microsoft Word document and deploy a minimal Apache web server to monitor communication from wherever someone opens the document.

 SEE: The goal is for the attacker to see an Office document in places they're likely to browse when pillaging the network.

 THINK: The attacker should think this document contains interesting or sensitive information about the company or its network.

 DO: When the attacker opens the document, we'll know they have been on the network, even if they've moved the document to a system we don't manage.

---

[1] Advertisers and marketers use web bugs extensively to check whether you've opened an email or attachment. This isn't a new idea, but one we'll certainly adopt for our honeydocs.

Configuring the Honeypot

Before creating the honeydoc, you'll need a web server to listen for connections from opened documents. We'll make that happen using a minimal Apache configuration[2]. Since it's likely attackers will pull files off your network before opening them, this server should be accessible from the public internet so the document HTTP request will reach the server for logging. Ideally, deploy the server away from your network infrastructure by using a cloud service such as Amazon EC2 or another host of your choosing. When you're ready, complete these steps on an Ubuntu system:

1. Install the apache2 package:

   ```
   sudo apt-get install apache2
   ```

2. If you've already explicitly enabled the system firewall, allow inbound access to port 80:

   ```
   sudo ufw allow 'Apache'
   ```

3. Create a directory for your domain. I'll identify this server with the generic and benign name 'update':

   ```
   sudo mkdir /var/www/update
   ```

4. Assign ownership of the directory to a non-root user:

   ```
   sudo chown -R $USER:$USER /var/www/update
   ```

5. Create an index page in the web directory:

   ```
   nano /var/www/update/index.html
   ```

6. You can put anything you like on this page, but keep in mind an attacker might eventually browse here. The web server serves this content when someone requests the webroot. A simple blank page is a good place to start:

   ```
   <html>
       <head>
           <title>Update Server</title>
       </head>
       <body></body>
   </html>
   ```

---

[2] You should spend some time securing your Apache server. The CIS benchmark provides a thorough guide: https://www.cisecurity.org/benchmark/apache_http_server/.

Create a new virtual host file:

```
sudo nano /etc/apache2/sites-available/update.conf
```

7. Insert the following block into the file, substituting appropriate values for the naming of your web server. Keep in mind that you'll use the URL in **ServerName** and **ServerAlias** to reach the server[3]. **DocumentRoot** should point to the directory you created in step 3.

```
<VirtualHost *:80>
    ServerAdmin me@chrissanders.org
    ServerName update.chrissanders.org
    ServerAlias update.chrissanders.org
    DocumentRoot /var/www/update
    ErrorLog ${APACHE_LOG_DIR}/error.log
    CustomLog ${APACHE_LOG_DIR}/access.log combined
</VirtualHost>
```

Enable the virtual host:

```
sudo a2ensite update.conf
```

8. Disable the default website:

```
sudo a2dissite 000-default.conf
```

9. Restart Apache:

```
sudo systemctl restart apache2
```

10. Verify the server is running by connecting to the ServerName URL in a browser. You should see a blank page with the Update Server title created in step 6.

With the server running, you'll need a custom URL for the honeydoc we're about to create. That should consist of the web server URL plus a token. For example, http://update.chrissanders.org/7cba9f2.

The string '7cba9f2' is a randomly generated token that doesn't have any meaning on its own. However, it does help you identify where an attacker is on your network because it's unique to a single document that ideally exists only in a single place. Of course, this requires you to keep track of which tokens are used in each document and where you've

---

[3] You'll need to ensure DNS is configured correctly so that the domain or subdomain points to the IP address of the web server. This is most likely configured with your domain registrar or hosting provider.

placed them. You can build references between honeydocs and tokens directly into detection rules. Still, I recommend maintaining a list in a spreadsheet to keep them all straight, as you might end up with several tokens. The token should be sufficiently unique so that you don't generate obnoxious false positives when monitoring for requests to the honey token URL.

Browsing to http://update.chrissanders.org/7cba9f2 (or whatever your version of this token is) yields an HTTP 404 Not Found response from the web server because nothing exists at that URL. That's perfectly fine for our use case. We don't want the honeydoc to render any real content, and the web server logs the request regardless of whether data exists at that location. Once someone opens the document and their system makes the request, you know there's evil afoot.

With the web server listening and a token link in hand, we're ready to configure the honeydoc. A honeydoc starts as a typical Office document that we'll modify to include a web bug. Follow these steps in Microsoft Word for Office 365 on a Windows 10 system[4].

1.   Create a new blank document or open an existing document.
2.   Click the **Insert** tab, select **Footer**, and choose one of the footer options to add the footer to the document. Or, if your document already has a footer, double click in the footer area to edit it. You can add the web bug anywhere, but I prefer the header or footer because it's less likely to be accidentally removed by changes made in other parts of the document.
3.   From the **Header & Footer** menu, select **Quick Parts** and **Field**.
4.   Select **IncludePicture** from the **Field names** list. Configure the following options (Figure 7-2) and click **OK**:
     •   In the **Filename or URL** textbox, type the token link created after setting up the web server.
     •   Enable the **Data not stored with document** and **Preserve formatting during updates** checkboxes.

---

[4] You can insert web bugs in all sorts of office documents across multiple platforms using the same technique, but the steps might vary slightly.

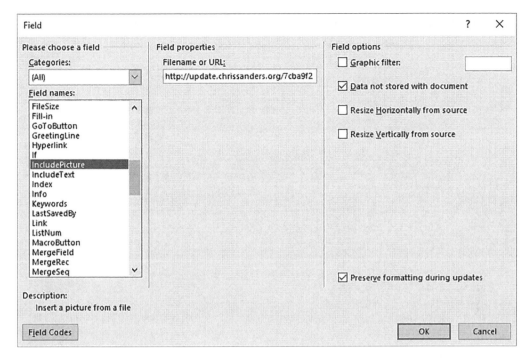

FIGURE 7-2:

Configuring the Web Bug

5. An empty picture box should load into the footer area. Double click it to switch to the **Picture Format** toolbar. Change the **Height** and **Width** options to .01". This change makes the web bug virtually invisible to the eye[5]. You can still select it by clicking and dragging your mouse over the area where it's located.

6. Save and close the document.

Whenever you open the document the next time, Word attempts to load the image from the remote URL, generating a request to your web server. Verify if the process worked by looking for an entry containing the token in **/var/log/apache2/access.log**. You've got yourself a functional honeydoc.

Discoverability

Attackers typically discover honeydocs while pillaging local drives and network shares after compromising individual hosts on a network. Depending on their level of access, they might open interesting documents upon discovery, or they might gather collections of materials for mass exfiltration to another host outside your control for later perusal.

---

[5] For another technique, select the Transparency option in the Picture Format toolbar and set the image to 100% transparency.

Either way, there's ample opportunity to make sure attackers stumble over honeydocs.

Honeydocs are most effective when they stand out amongst other files. Using enticing file names is the easiest way to achieve uniqueness. There are quite a few ways to approach honeydoc naming, but you should strive to appeal to things attackers are interested in. Table 7-1 has a few examples, but you should customize these to your environment.

Attacker's Interest	Description	Examples
Network details	Information like user lists, network diagrams, and configuration details might help the attacker further their hold on the network.	system.xlsx finance_users.docx network_overview.pptx
Intellectual property	Sensitive data related to market offerings might help some attackers achieve their mission goals.	suppliers.xlsx customers.docx chemical_synthesizing_process.pptx
Personal information	Attackers seeking to harm reputations will often look for information about individuals or information that might allow further compromise into an individual's personal, non-work accounts.	employee_complaints.xlsx bob_smith_employee_info.docx direct_deposit_stephanie_clark.docx passwords.docx

TABLE 7-1:

Example honeydoc naming techniques

There are a few other simple strategies you can employ to help your file stand out. These are subtle, but their additive effect is quite powerful at enticing attackers to open the honeydoc:

- Use document types unique from those around them—for example, a spreadsheet in a folder full of text documents.
- Use unique or odd file sizes. For example, a 23 MB Word document stands out from bunches of documents less than 1 MB in size.
- Experiment with unique capitalization. An all-caps document name draws attention when other documents are lower or mixed case.
- Place files within their own directories.

Keep in mind that there is such a thing as trying too hard[6]. If your honeydoc tries to be everything, it might end up looking too good to be true and achieve nothing. Lean on using multiple honeydocs with different naming and placement strategies rather than a single honeydoc that pulls out all the stops.

Because honeydocs are relatively trivial to create and deploy, there's no reason you can't litter them in multiple places spanning common folders and sensitive assets. The most common locations are in local document folders on individual workstations or network shares mapped from workstations.

There's also value in placing them in internal web server directories. For example, attackers often look for vulnerable WordPress sites by scanning the wp-admin/ directory. If you place a honeydoc here, attackers are likely to discover it and may open it to see what they've found. That doesn't necessarily mean the attacker compromised the web server, but it could indicate their attempt at lateral movement from another compromised host.

One last strategy includes attaching honeydocs to email messages within the mailboxes of users. Attackers frequently target mailboxes and perform searches for relevant keywords. If an attacker discovers and opens a honeydoc through this process, you know they've compromised at least one user's mailbox[7].

Remember that legitimate users are more likely to trigger honeydocs as you make them more visible. There's a delicate balance here to deceive attackers while not overwhelming yourself with false positives from misguided users. I often have the most luck achieving that balance by placing honeydocs in their own folders. Legitimate users are less likely to both open an unknown folder and a file, while attackers' motivations generally push them to open both. If a user does open a honeydoc, the good news is that most won't make a mistake with the same document more than once after a stern but friendly counseling session with someone on the security team[8]. It's also easy to verify whether a legitimate user opened the file with a simple phone call.

When you deploy honeydocs in multiple locations, you don't just have several potential places to detect adversaries. You also spawn the ability to track their movements. Imagine a scenario where an attacker opens a document on a finance user's workstation, and a few hours later opens one on a server only accessible by the research team. You now know something about that attacker's path, and can start piecing together a timeline

---

[6] If you don't believe me, you should have seen how much hair gel I used in high school.

[7] You can do this on a small scale for your own protection by sending yourself an email and storing it in a mailbox folder.

[8] You'll have more sympathy for your users when you accidentally open your own honeydocs. I won't admit to how many times I did that while writing this book over several months.

of events connecting these two unrelated systems. Every point on the timeline that a honeydoc gives you speeds along the investigation. Deploy honeydocs with variety across your network to reap their full benefits.

Interactivity

Most honeydocs won't provide any more interactivity than their native applications usually allow. That's to say that an Excel spreadsheet will act like, well . . . an Excel spreadsheet. So, there's not much to consider for interactivity beyond that. However, a little extra effort might suppress attacker discovery of your deception strategy and can help you use honeydocs as breadcrumbs to other honeypots for attacker movement tracking inside your network perimeter.

When creating your honeydoc earlier, I said that you could start with a blank document or work from something that already exists. A blank document still opens and still triggers the web bug, so that's all the interaction you need to meet the goal of the honeydoc. But, it might arouse suspicions in the attacker and scare them off or cause a change in tradecraft. This event isn't 'game over' because you'll still know the attacker is there, but you might hope to gather more information before they know you're on the hunt. While attacker awareness of the honeydoc is unlikely, you can mitigate some of this by attempting to make your document's contents resemble what its name indicates it should contain.

A more realistic looking document also allows an opportunity to leverage other honeypots. In the next chapter, I'll talk about honey credentials, or usernames and passwords created solely for attackers to discover and use. You can insert honey credentials into honey documents and wait to see where the attacker attempts to use them. Because the credentials don't work, they won't allow access that causes harm, but it can help you determine the extent of the attacker's compromise.

NOTE: *Office applications are extremely powerful when you consider their ability to execute code through the use of macros. Attackers use macros to compromise networks all the time, so you might be tempted to include macro-executed code in your honeydocs to expand your detection and attacker profiling capabilities. That's a useful strategy, and there is no shortage of clever examples you can use to trick the attacker into enabling macros just like they might have done to your users. However, beware of the slippery slope of using macros to execute code and cause some negative retribution at the expense of your attacker's computer. This tactic is inadvisable for a few reasons. First, you never know where the attacker might open the document and you could cause harm to one of your systems, or another legitimate entity where the attacker chooses to stage your files after exfiltration. Second, even though you might feel morally vindicated by attacking the attacker, this could constitute a crime and leave you on the wrong side of the law.*

Monitoring

Since web bugs communicate with a web server, we rely on those web server logs for alerting when attackers open honeydocs. If you followed the process I outlined earlier to set up an Apache web server, you'll get honeydoc logs in /var/log/apache2/access.log. Those logs look like this:

```
172.16.16.178 - - [15/Apr/2020:19:19:47 +0000] "GET /j2b4je2bd HTTP/1.1"
404 498 "-" "Mozilla/4.0 (compatible; ms-office; MSOffice 16)"
```

The Apache combined access log format provides some useful information to help direct the investigation:

- Timestamp (15/Apr/2020:19:19:47 +0000): When the attacker opened the document. Use this to plot a point on your investigation timeline.
- Source IP Address (172.16.16.178): The IP address where the attacker opened the document. This address could be the system where the document was hosted, another internal system the attacker controls, or an external system indicating an attacker exfiltrated the document.
- User Agent (Mozilla/4.0 (compatible; ms-office; MSOffice 16)): The user agent string provided by the application that opened the document.
- HTTP Request (GET /j2b4je2bd HTTP/1.1): The request contains the token, so you know which honeydoc the attacker accessed.

These logs should be paired with detection rules to alert analysts when honeydoc access occurs. Here's a Sigma rule that alerts on log entries containing any of the listed tokens[9]:

```
title: Honeydoc Web Bug Triggered
description: A web bug triggered when a honeydoc was opened.
date: 2020/01/01
tags:
    - honeypot
author: Chris Sanders
logsource:
    product: honeytoken
    service: office_honeydoc
detection:
    selection:
        request_line|contains:
            -   'token1'
            -   'token2'
```

---

[9] Make sure to replace token1, token2, etc. with your actual token values.

```
        -   'token3'
    condition: selection
fields:
    -   "Source IP"
    -   "User Agent"
    -   "HTTP Request"
falsepositives:
    - User Errors
level: high
```

Since you'll likely have several tokens tied to unique honeydocs, you can choose to create individual alerts for each one matching the token string itself from the log, or simply use a rule as I've shown above that alerts on any token match. A strategy that I've grown fond of is categorizing tokens based on their deployment characteristics and building individual rules based on those token features. For example, I'll configure tokens to include subdirectories that imply specific meaning:

- `<server name>/id1/<token>`: Tokens deployed in workstations or file shares
- `<server name>/id2/<token>`: Tokens deployed on sensitive servers
- `<server name>/id3/<token>`: Tokens deployed in mailboxes

I base alert signatures on the category the token falls into, matching "id1", "id2", or "id3" for each grouping. In my example, I've grouped tokens by their type of deployment, but you can also group them by network segment, department, specific responding analyst groups, or anything else that makes sense for your workflow.

Going Further

While I showed you how to set up honeytokens from scratch, Thinkst (the makers of the OpenCanary tool that I demonstrated in the previous chapter) provides both a service and open source tool to aid in honeytoken deployment. You can generate honeydocs on the fly using the Canarytoken service (Figure 7-3)[10], and they'll provide the server infrastructure to receive the web bug call back and send you alert notifications by email or webhook.

---

[10] This is a free service found at https://canarytokens.org/. Notice that they provide honeytokens for many more file types beyond office documents!

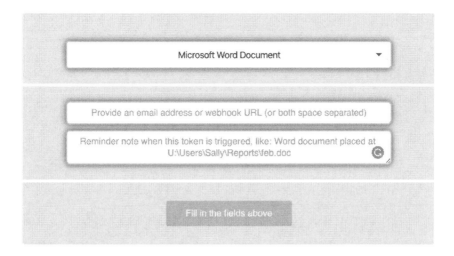

FIGURE 7-3:

Automated honeydoc generation provided by Thinkst Canarytoken

The code that powers the Canarytoken service is available freely on GitHub[11]. You can deploy it within your network and connect it to more appropriate logging sources within your environment. If you're comfortable with Python, you can even build automation around these techniques. For an added challenge, take a look at msword.py in the Canarytoken GitHub repo and try to reverse engineer how Microsoft Word represents web bugs in XML!

FROM THE TRENCHES:

A colleague in the medical industry told me an interesting story about how honey tokens helped her avoid a HIPAA violation. She suspected that the company they shipped outdated computers to wasn't doing their due diligence to wipe the hard drives before reselling the systems. As a test, she reinstalled the operating system on a few computers and configured auto-logon for them. Whenever they booted up, a VBscript invoked a web bug that sent a request to a web server she owned. After sending them to the vendor, every system immediately triggered the web bug and then went dark for about a month. Then, over the course of several weeks, each one started triggering the web bug frequently from IP addresses resolving to internet provider ranges. The vendor was, indeed, reselling the computers without wiping the hard drives.

---

[11] Download Canarytokens at https://github.com/thinkst/canarytokens. For quicker setup, consider deploying Canarytokens using docker images from https://github.com/thinkst/canarytokens-docker.

Honey Files

Another way to deploy honeytokens is with benign files paired with robust monitoring capabilities from the host operating system. This strategy extends your ability to use honey tokens with any file, even if it's not an Office document.

A *honey file* is any file paired with interaction logging for the exclusive purpose of intrusion detection. As an example, I'll show you how to pair any file with the Microsoft Windows file access auditing capability to create a honey file (Figure 7-4).

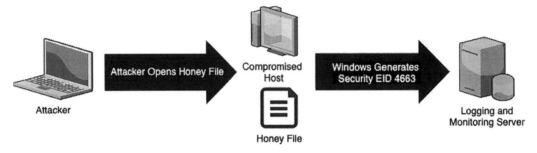

FIGURE 7-4:

A Windows honey file relies on built-in monitoring capabilities

 SEE: The goal is for the attacker to see a file in places they're likely to browse when pillaging the network.

 THINK: The attacker should think this file contains interesting or sensitive information about the company or its network.

 DO: When the attacker interacts with the file in ways we specify, we'll know they are on the network.

Configuring the Honeypot

The beauty of this example is that you can use any file you like, whether it's an executable, PDF, image, or something custom to your environment. The file has no unique properties other than the metadata (name, size, location) that you'll use to track it. Otherwise, Windows auditing does the hard work.

We'll start by enabling the appropriate object access group policy setting. For a single system (not part of a domain) hosting a honey file, follow these steps:

1. Access the **Local Security Policy** from the **Windows Administrative Tools** folder on the Start Menu
2. Browse to **Advanced Audit Policy Configuration > System Audit Policies**

– Local Group Policy Object > Object Access

3. Double click **Audit File System**
4. Place a checkmark next to **Configure the following audit events:** and **Success** (Figure 7-5).
5. Click **OK** and close the policy editor

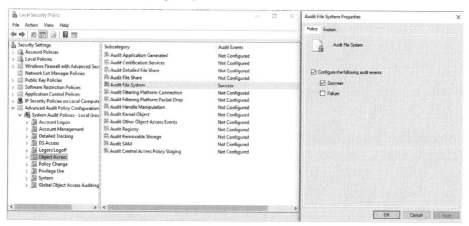

FIGURE 7-5:

Enabling file auditing policy on a single system

For a system or group of systems hosting honey files in Windows domain, follow these steps:

1. Access the **Group Policy Management** tool from the **Administrative Tools** folder on the Start Menu.
2. Right-click the Organizational Unit containing the systems that will host honey files and select **Create a GPO in this domain and link it here . . .**
3. Provide a name for the policy and click **OK**.
4. Right-click the new policy and select **Edit**.
5. Browse to **Computer Configuration > Policies > Windows Settings > Security Settings > Advanced Audit Policy Configuration > Audit Policies > Object Access.**
6. Double click **Audit File System.**
7. Place a checkmark next to **Configure the following audit events:** and **Success**.
8. Click **OK** and close the policy editor. This policy will take a couple of hours to take effect on domain member systems, but if you need to expedite this process for testing on an individual system you can run **gpupdate /force** from the command line.

With the group policy configured, you're ready to create the honey file and configure auditing. You'll complete these steps on the system housing the honey file:

1. Create a new file or pick an existing file and place it in a directory an attacker is likely to encounter once they gain a foothold on the network or that specific system.

2. Right-click the file and choose **Properties**. Browse to the **Security** tab, click **Advanced**, followed by the **Auditing** tab. Click **Continue**, and provide administrative credentials if requested.

3. Click **Add** to create a new auditing entry. First, you'll select the users for which the audit applies. Click **Select a principal** and choose the user or group. I generally use the Authenticated Users group. In the **Type** drop-down, select **Success**.

4. Click the **Show advanced permissions** link to show all the audit actions available. You can experiment with these, but some can be quite noisy. I usually stick with **List folder/read data** and **Delete**[12] (Figure 7-6).

5. Click **OK** on each open window to close the file property dialogs.

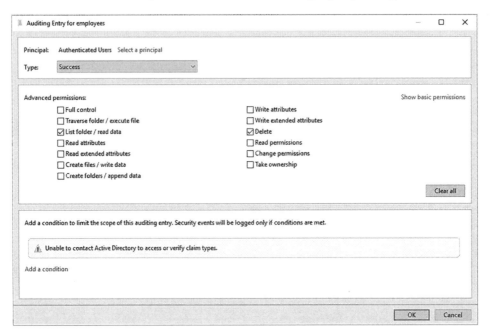

FIGURE 7-6:

Enabling auditing on a single honey file

Now, whenever someone opens the honey file, you'll see Windows Event ID 4663 indicating file system object access in the system's local security log. We'll talk more about

---

[12] These will also catch file copies and renames.

that log entry in the monitoring section in a little while.

If you're dealing with multiple honey files, configuring auditing settings on them one at a time might be tedious and labor-intensive. The audit_honeyfile.ps1 PowerShell script automates the process I enumerated above:

```
# This script sets the auditing policy for a honey file.
# Adapted from Aaron Giuoco's Blog: http://giuoco.org/security/configure-
file-and-registry-auditing-with-powershell/

function AddAuditToFile {
    param
    (
        [Parameter(Mandatory=$true)]
        [string]$path
    )

    Get-Acl $path -Audit | Format-List Path,AuditToString | Out-File
-FilePath 'file_before.txt' -Width 200 -Append
    $File_ACL = Get-Acl $path
    $AccessRule = New-Object System.Security.
AccessControl.FileSystemAuditRule("Authenticated
Users","ReadData,Delete","none","none","Success")
    $File_ACL.AddAuditRule($AccessRule)
    $File_ACL | Set-Acl $path
    Get-Acl $path -Audit | Format-List Path,AuditToString | Out-File
-FilePath 'file_after.txt' -Width 200 -Append
}

for ( $i = 0; $i -lt $args.count; $i++ ) {
    AddAuditToFile $args[$i]
 }
```

Run this script using PowerShell by providing the file name of the file you wish to audit as an argument.

```
PS C:\Users\sanders> .\audit_honeyfile.ps1 auditme.txt
```

You can supply multiple file names in a single command execution. Be sure to run the script from the context of a user with permission to modify the target file privileges. The script also produces two output files: file_before.txt records the auditing settings before making changes, and file_after.txt records them after the change. These can be useful for troubleshooting or reverting changes if you overwrite something important.

Don't forget to document where you deploy honey files! Create a list of each file, its properties, and location. Store that list in a secure place where attackers aren't likely to discover it.

Discoverability

All the same discovery rules apply for honey files as they did for honeydocs. However, you should take special care to consider the type of source file used for your honey file and where its placement makes the most sense. For example, an image file named alek.png will stand out if it's on an industrial control server that manipulates circuit breakers. That's not a bad thing if you want the file to stand out. However, it might be challenging to place the file in a folder where it's likely to get discovered on this type of server. You must be mindful of both how likely the attacker is to find the location of the file, and how likely they are to notice it amongst other files in that location.

Before moving on, I want to show you another trick to lure attackers to honey files while limiting legitimate user exposure—hidden mapped drives, or for our purposes, honey drives. Attackers know that much of the sensitive information held by a company is collaborative. Users contribute to shared databases, spreadsheets, and other sorts of files on shared resources. For simple collaborative files and documents, that sharing is most frequently accomplished with drives mapped from workstations to shared folders on servers. Therefore, when attackers compromise workstations they often move quickly to enumerate and access mapped drives.

Mapping a drive is pretty straightforward. From an interactive desktop, browse to a shared folder on a server, right-click it, choose Map network drive, pick a drive letter, and you're done. Alternatively, you can achieve the same result on the command line using the net tool, like this:

```
net use X: \\server\folder\
```

The mapped drive's presence is enough to entice the attacker over, where a honey file will be waiting[13]. However, legitimate users are likely to notice the mapped drive as well, given the drive's prominent display in Windows Explorer. Even though there's no reason for the user to access this particular shared folder, it could result in false positive alerts. Fortunately, there's a simple registry hack that'll hide the drive letter from Explorer:

1. Open the registry editor by launching **regedit.exe** from the search bar or command prompt.
2. Browse to **HKEY_LOCAL_MACHINE\Software\Microsoft\Windows\CurrentVersion\Policies\ Explorer**.
3. Right-click on the Explorer folder, hover over **New** and select **DWORD (32-bit) Value**.

---

[13] You don't have to use a real shared folder for this strategy since the drive itself is a breadcrumb. You can create a shared folder to house honey files just for this purpose.

4. Name the value **NoDrives**.

5. Under **Base**, select the **Decimal** option (Figure 7-7). Enter the appropriate value for the drive letter you wish to hide from Table 7-2 below.

Letter	DWORD	Letter	DWORD	Letter	DWORD
A	1	J	512	S	262144
B	2	K	1024	T	524288
C	4	L	2048	U	1048576
D	8	M	4096	V	2097152
E	16	N	8192	W	4194304
F	32	O	16384	X	8388608
G	64	P	32788	Y	16777216
H	128	Q	65536	Z	33554432
I	256	R	131072		

TABLE 7-2:

ASCII to 32-bit DWORD decimal codes for hiding drives

6. Click OK. You can make the change take effect by restarting Explorer in the Task Manager or restarting the system.

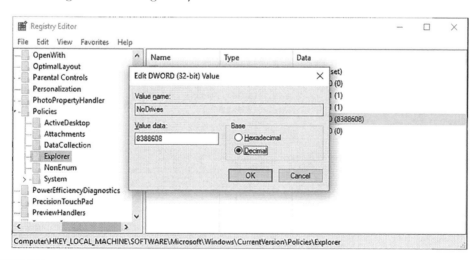

FIGURE 7-7:

Modifying the registry to hide a mapped network drive

After the change has taken effect, the mapped drive won't be visible in Explorer. However, attackers can still access it through the command prompt or by typing it into the Explorer address bar manually. Now, legitimate users are less likely to stumble across the drive, which still lures attackers navigating from the command line[14].

Interactivity

In general, the honey file won't provide much interactivity. Ideally, it functions as the file type it represents (a ZIP file will unzip, a PDF will open in a PDF reader, etc.). But otherwise, there's no expectation for the file to provide more interactivity. You do, once again, have an opportunity to drop breadcrumbs to other honeypots within the file where appropriate.

Monitoring

An attacker accessing the honey file unknowingly generates Windows Event ID 4663 (Figure 7-8).

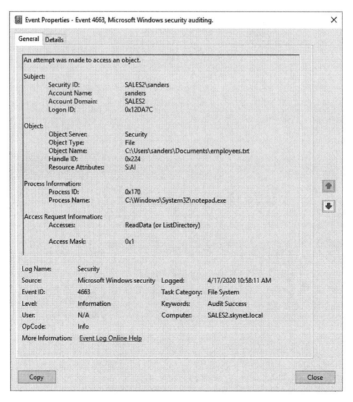

FIGURE 7-8:

Windows EID 4688 Indicates Honey File Access

---

[14] If you want to be like me, test this before you deploy it in production. If you want to be better than me, don't forget to remove your test registry key so you don't get confused about why you're missing a network drive when you need it later.

Event ID: 4663

Provider: Microsoft-Windows-Security-Auditing.

Event Description: An attempt was made to access an object.

Behavior: This event reports attempts to access objects for which you've enabled auditing.

Enablement: For this log to be generated, Object Access Monitoring must be enabled, as described earlier in this chapter.

Investigative Details:

- **Logged/Timestamp**: When the attacker accessed the document. Use this to plot a point on your investigation timeline.
- **Object Name** [ObjectName]: The path and file accessed. This should be your honey file.
- **Computer** [Computer]: The system where the document is stored.
- **Account Name** [SubjectUserName]: The user account that accessed the document.
- **Process Name** [ProcessName]: The process that accessed the document. This process might indicate the level of access the attacker has. For example, cmd.exe for command line access or notepad.exe for desktop access. This value won't be present if someone accesses the file from a remote system (such as through a mapped drive).
- **Process ID** [ProcessId]: The hexadecimal representation of the PID from the process that accessed the file.
- **Accesses** [AccessMask]: The type of access to the file[15]. For example, ReadData to view the contents of the file or Delete to remove it.

This Sigma rule alerts when someone accesses a honey file:

```
title: Windows Honeydoc Accessed
description: A user read, deleted, copied, or moved a Honeydoc on a
Windows system.
date: 2020/01/01
tags:
    - honeypot
author: Chris Sanders
logsource:
    product: windows
```

---

[15] These are represented as hexadecimal values when viewing raw log data. See a full list here: https://docs.microsoft.com/en-us/windows/security/threat-protection/auditing/event-4663.

```
    service: security
detection:
    selection:
        EventID: 4663
        Object Name: %HONEYPOT_PATH_AND_FILE_NAMES_HERE%[16]
    filter:
        Process Name: %COMMON_FALSE_POSITIVES_FROM_PROCESSES%
    condition: selection and not filter
fields:
    -   "Object Name"
    -   "Computer"
    -   "Account Name"
    -   "Process Name"
    -   "Process ID"
    -   "Accesses"
falsepositives:
    - System Processes
    - User Errors
level: high
```

This rule might be noisy at first. For example, viewing the file properties of a honey file with this logging configuration generates multiple log entries, so aggregating alerts by process or file name can be helpful. Also, legitimate applications (malware scanners) and system processes (the Search Indexer) might access the document in ways that aren't related to attacker movement. You should exclude these processes from the detection rule by adding them to the filter section.

If your tolerance for working your way through these false positives is low initially, you can limit the scope of the rule to only generate alerts if someone accesses the honey file using a likely process, for example only alerting on access to a DOCX file from winword.exe, cmd.exe, and explorer.exe. While this covers a lot of use cases and decreases false positives, you limit detection opportunities if an attacker comes up with something creative. For example, the rule would not generate an alert if an attacker used a PowerShell script to copy the file to another location.

Lastly, keep in mind that monitoring honey files relies on logs generated by a system that an attacker might already control. That level of control means they could clear the system logs, or stop the logging service from running. You can mitigate the former by shipping logs to a remote collector, which you're likely already doing in an enterprise environment. The latter probably means you aren't going to see log entries related to your honeypot, so you should rely on other detection for monitoring the Windows event logging service.

---

[16] You could also only include the file name, but make sure it's unique to limit false positives.

Going Farther

We've now discussed two methods to use files as tokens, both by embedding web bugs in Office documents and pairing Windows file access auditing with individual files. So, why not use these techniques together on the same files? The only reason this might cause you grief is through the generation of multiple alerts for the same file access. Given the alert volume should still be pretty low, that isn't too big of a deal. So, if you'd like some deception in depth, then that should work perfectly fine.

While you're at it, know that Windows auditing techniques described in this section also work on folders and registry keys. For both of those, you can edit their properties and assign auditing entries just like we did with files. That gives you a few more honey tokens to play around with!

Honey Folders

You can apply the same auditing policy from the last section to folders. However, folders also provide a unique trick of their own by leveraging a built-in Windows Explorer feature. For this honeypot, we'll create a folder exclusively for intrusion detection that generates an alert when accessed (Figure 7-9).

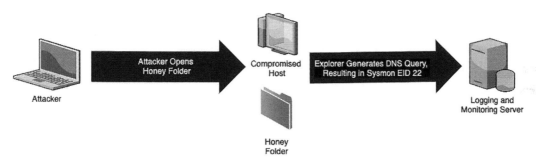

FIGURE 7-9:

A honey folder alerts when someone browses to it or its parent

 SEE: The goal is for the attacker to see a folder on a system they've compromised.

 THINK: The attacker should think the folder contains interesting or sensitive information about the company or its network.

 DO: When the attacker accesses the folder, we'll know they are on the network.

Configuring the Honeypot

To create honey folders, we'll leverage a Windows INI file trick. Windows INI files have been around for a long time and are typically just text-based configuration files for the operating system or applications. Some INI files have special functions when they take on certain properties in specific folder locations. For example, Windows automatically creates a hidden file named Desktop.ini in most folders on a system. This file contains information and settings about that folder and how you interact with it. Among Desktop.ini's capabilities, you can set a custom icon image for the folder that's visible in Windows Explorer. That's not interesting by itself, but the feature becomes valuable for detection when you learn that you can set that custom icon image location to a UNC path and you can leverage DNS domain names within that path. Now, whenever an attacker opens a folder containing an "enhanced" Desktop.ini or its parent folder, the system generates a DNS query to attempt to resolve the domain referenced in the file, which you'll monitor for alerting.

To get started with a honey folder, first identify a directory location an attacker is likely to discover during compromises, such as a local documents folder or a shared public drive (Figure 7-10).

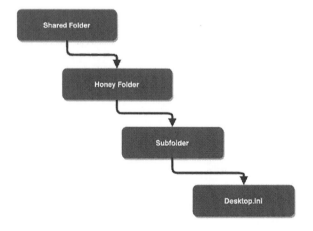

FIGURE 7-10:

The Honey Drive directory structure

Complete the following steps while working from that location:

1. Create an enticingly named folder. For example, "Financial Reports."
2. Within that folder, create a subfolder. The name of the subfolder doesn't matter as much because, by the time the attacker sees it, they'll likely have already tripped an alert.

3. Open notepad and type the following:

```
[.ShellClassInfo]
IconResource=\\%USERNAME%.%COMPUTERNAME%.%USERDOMAIN%.jc18.
update.chrissanders.org\image
```

4. Replace **update.chrissanders.org** with a domain name you control. The **jc18** portion of the domain is the unique token identifying the specific honey folder and can be anything you like.

5. Save the file into the subfolder as **Desktop.ini**.

6. Open a command prompt from the Start Menu or by typing **cmd.exe** from the Start Menu search bar. Issue the following command to set the system property on the subfolder:

```
attrib +s subfolder
```

7. While still in the command prompt, enter this command to set the system and hidden properties on the Desktop.ini file:

```
attrib +s +h subfolder/Desktop.ini
```

8. Close the command prompt.

Now, whenever someone browses to the directory you've created, Windows attempts to resolve the domain name from Desktop.ini with a DNS query. I'll show you how to configure DNS logging to capture this traffic in just a bit, but you can verify things are working now by using a packet capture tool, such as Wireshark (Figure 7-11)[17].

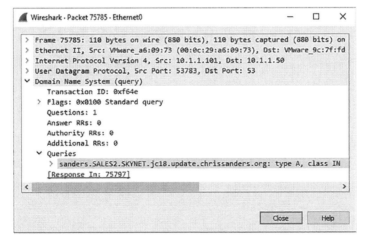

---

[17] Presumably, an attacker with control of a system could also intercept these packets. However, they'll be buried in other traffic and the link between the DNS communication and browsing the folder won't be clear.

FIGURE 7-11:

Wireshark shows DNS traffic representing access to a honey folder

Once again, be sure and document which token maps to which honey folder and where that honey folder resides.

Discoverability

Once again, all the same naming suggestions I've described in the honeydocs section earlier apply to naming honey folders. You're a bit more limited with folders since you can't play around with file extensions or sizes. Still, from my experience, attackers are more likely to open interestingly named folders than files, simply because folder opening provides instant validation and isn't typically logged.

Interactivity

All a folder should do is provide access to whatever is inside, so that's all a honey folder needs to do as well. Keep in mind that the strategy I've described here only works if an attacker interacts with a folder through Windows Explorer. If they access a honey folder from the command line, Desktop.ini won't come into play, and the system won't generate a DNS request for alerting.

Monitoring

The strategy I've outlined for deploying honey folders results in a DNS query generated from a host whenever an attacker browses to the folder. There are a few ways you can log this data, but we'll start with host-based DNS logging on Windows. This technique is the preferred mechanism in most cases, particularly if you've configured your clients to resolve DNS from an internal host that isn't crossing a network sensor boundary.

Traditionally, Windows DNS logging has been a scourge to detection engineers because it's difficult to parse, doesn't always provide enough relevant information, and is relatively inflexible in its configuration. So, I'm not going to cover it in depth here[18]. Instead, I recommend you leverage the Microsoft Sysinternals Sysmon tool, which extends Windows' security logging capability and includes more robust DNS logging. You can learn more about Sysmon, including how to run it here: https://docs.microsoft.com/en-us/sysinternals/downloads/sysmon.

You'll need Sysmon installed on either the system where the attacker opens the

---

[18] Alas, if you must go this route, start here: https://docs.microsoft.com/en-us/previous-versions/windows/it-pro/windows-server-2012-r2-and-2012/dn800669(v=ws.11).

honey folder or the server resolving the DNS queries for that system[19]. Sysmon functions according to settings in an XML configuration file[20]. The following configuration file enables DNS logging, but only for domains ending with chrissanders.org:

```
<Sysmon schemaversion="4.22">
 <EventFiltering>
  <DnsQuery onmatch="include">
      <QueryName condition="end with">chrissanders.org</QueryName>
  </DnsQuery>
 </EventFiltering>
</Sysmon>
```

Here, I've chosen to only log data for the domain I'm using for my honey folders by using the onmatch="include" configuration. I've done this because logging every DNS query is noisy, and for now, this gets us the logs we want. Once applied, interaction with the honey folder generates Event ID 22 (Figure 7-12) in the Sysmon Operational log:

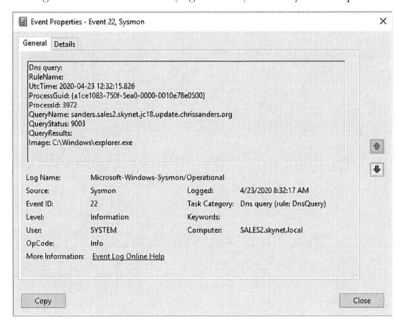

FIGURE 7-12:

Sysmon DNS logging indicates honey folder interaction

---

[19] Sysmon DNS logging is not available for Windows 7 and earlier versions.

[20] If you're new to Sysmon, I recommend starting with SwiftonSecurity's config. It's configured with "bang for your buck" efficiency in mind and is a great jumping off point: https://github.com/SwiftOnSecurity/sysmon-config.

Event ID: 22

Provider: Microsoft-Windows-Sysmon.

Event Description: DNS Query.

Behavior: This event reports when a process generates a DNS query.

Investigative Details:

- **UtcTime/Timestamp**: When the attacker accessed the folder. Use this to plot a point on your investigation timeline.
- **Query Name** [QueryName]: The domain name queried. This value comes from Desktop.ini, and includes system variables identified there[21]:
    - %USERNAME% – The username accessing the folder.
    - %COMPUTERNAME% – The computer name where the folder was accessed from.
    - %USERDOMAIN% – The domain name of the user accessing the folder.
    - jc18.update.chrissanders.org – The domain name (with subdomain as a token) we specified.
- **Computer** [Computer]: The system that generated the DNS query.

This Sigma rule alerts when someone accesses a honey folder:

```
title: Windows Honey Folder Accessed
description: Someone browsed to a honey folder on a Windows system
date: 2020/01/01
tags:
    - honeypot
author: Chris Sanders
logsource:
    product: windows
    service: sysmon
detection:
    selection:
        EventID: 22
    QueryName: *%HONEYPOT_DOMAIN_HERE%
    condition: selection
fields:
    - "QueryName"
    - "Computer"
falsepositives:
```

---

[21] Because this additional information appears as part of a DNS subdomain, you'll want to verify that these logs are parsed correctly if you pull them into a log aggregator.

```
    - User Errors
level: high
```

If you're using external DNS resolvers and can't monitor DNS queries on the host level, you can monitor their transmission across the network with an IDS. The following Suricata rule detects an outbound DNS query matching the domain configured in the honey folder's Desktop.ini file:

```
alert dns $HOME_NET any -> $EXTERNAL_DNS_SERVERS 53 (msg:"Windows Honey
Folder Accessed"; dns.query; content:"update.chrissanders.org"; nocase;
classtype:honeypot; sid:50000001; rev:1;)
```

This signature alerts on any DNS query (**alert dns**) from an internal IP address (**$HOME_NET any**) to an external DNS resolver (**$EXTERNAL_DNS_SERVERS**). The list of external DNS servers referenced in the signature should contain whatever DNS server you've configured your endpoints to use. The signature only alerts if the query includes update.chrissanders.org, which is used exclusively for honey folder DNS (**dns.query; content: "update.chrissanders.org"; nocase;**).

Keep in mind that systems cache DNS entries for a short while. During this time, subsequent browsing to the honey folder won't generate logs or alerts because the system is relying on its cache.

Conclusion

In this chapter, I've demonstrated three approaches for deploying honey tokens. The honeydoc technique used a web bug embedded in an Office document to alert when an attacker opens the file. The honey file technique used Microsoft object access auditing to generate Windows alerts when an attacker viewed files of our choosing. The final method, honey folders, leveraged a Windows Explorer trick to generate DNS queries for alerting when attackers browsed to specific folders.

The use cases for these techniques overlap, but their varying discoverability, interactivity, and monitoring characteristics make them useful in different attack scenarios. By layering each method, you create an in-depth ecosystem of deception that provides more opportunities to catch attackers on the network and track their movements as they expand their reach. Honey tokens are easy to deploy and manage, which makes them my favorite honeypot technique to get started with.

HONEY CREDENTIALS 8

WHILE AN ATTACKER'S GOALS MOST COMMONLY HINGE on accessing data, that access often comes through leveraging legitimate user credentials. You don't need to worry about exploits and vulnerabilities when you can access things as authorized users do. Even when credentials aren't used to gain an initial foothold into a network, attackers aggressively seek them to further their sphere of control over networked assets en route to an objective. It's no surprise that an abundance of techniques exists for stealing them.

As defenders, we can use the attacker's desire for credentials to our advantage by giving them away freely. *Honey credentials* are fake login credentials designed to lure attackers into attempting authentication to a service. Of course, the attackers don't know the credentials are fake. Instead, when they try to login with them, we'll know we've got foxes in the hen house. Honey credentials are another form of honey tokens, but they're valuable and versatile enough that they deserve their own chapter.

In this chapter, I'll describe methods for using honey credentials to deceive attackers by mimicking accounts for legitimate services on your network. I'll mostly focus on techniques to distribute those credentials so that they're likely to be discovered by typical attacker tradecraft. I'll describe strategies for leveraging LSA secrets with honey token services, injecting credentials into process memory, and configuring LLMNR honey broadcasts.

Honey Credential and Service Interaction

All honey credentials take the same basic approach. The attacker finds them, has a sense of where to use them, and tries to. You'll leverage whatever authentication monitoring you already use for that service to know when that happens (Figure 8-1).

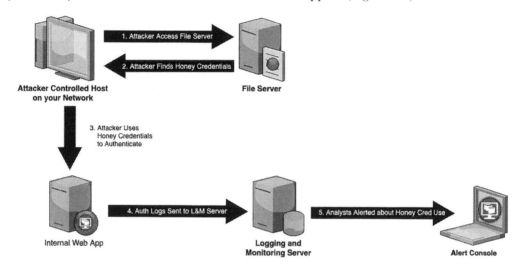

FIGURE 8-1:

Attackers discover honey credentials and attempt to authenticate with them

The goal for most forms of honey credentials is for the attacker to see credentials when attempting to harvest them from the network, or by happenstance while pillaging parts of the network they've already compromised. They should think these credentials provide some form of authorized access to a service, but we'll know they're on the network when they attempt to authenticate using the pilfered credentials. These goals remain fairly consistent, but I'll define them more specifically as they relate to each honeypot technique described in this chapter.

Attackers place the most value on credentials they know how to use and that leads them closer to a goal. Their knowledge of how to use credentials depends primarily on the context from which they've stolen them. For example, an attacker finds a document in a user's personal network folder containing credentials alongside the URL to a web server. It's reasonably apparent they'll use that username and password to attempt authentication to the web server. Separately, an attacker harvests honey credentials from a database through SQL injection. They know that those credentials associate with the very web server they've used to orchestrate their attack so far.

To make honey credentials seem valuable, use credentials relevant to more sensitive assets. That probably includes your Windows domain, cloud infrastructure, application servers, and databases. Remember, you're assuming an attacker is already in your network and seeking to further their sphere of control or move closer to some goal. Having more compromised accounts on a Windows domain helps attackers find and pillage more sensitive information. At the same time, credentials to a supplier management tool help attackers concerned with intellectual property learn more about your manufacturing processes. If you understand what's valuable on your network, you'll appreciate what attackers might target.

The easiest way to ensure that attackers find credentials is by leaving them around in clear text form. Unfortunately, users often jot down passwords to network resources so they won't forget them. Even at times when this is a temporary measure, they often forget to clean up after themselves. Attackers know this, so they look for remnants of credentials scattered across compromised network assets. This means attackers are likely to discover cleartext honey credentials placed in:

- Local documents folders
- Public shared folders
- Mapped drives
- Code repositories

Keep in mind that credentials aren't just usernames and passwords. They can take the form of certificates, API keys, SSH keys, cloud service keys, and hashes. Regardless of the format, honey credentials generally don't allow successful authentication to legitimate assets. In the rest of this chapter, we'll look at more specific examples of how you might use honey credentials.

Honey Token Service

Many of the times attackers compromise individual systems, they are relegated to the limited access of the user account they've commandeered. There are numerous techniques they might use to expand their access, but they often revolve around accessing credentials to other accounts already stored on the machine. One place these credentials exist on Windows machines is within the Local Security Authority (LSA) secrets, particularly as it pertains to service accounts.

Whenever administrators install services manually on a system, they often create accounts to run them. This strategy requires that they provide the username and password to that account on the system running the service, which is stored in the LSA secrets cache in the registry's security hive at *SECURITY\Policy\Secrets*. While you can't just open up the registry and view this information due to specific protection mechanisms, there are a few tools and techniques attackers use to read this data successfully. Doing so provides service account credentials in cleartext.

Knowing that attackers seek credentials with this technique, we'll use this to our advantage by creating a honey token service (not to be confused with the broader category of honey services). This honey token service won't start automatically, but we'll configure it to run under the context of a user account created just for this purpose. However, the password we'll provide doesn't let the account authenticate successfully (Figure 8-2).

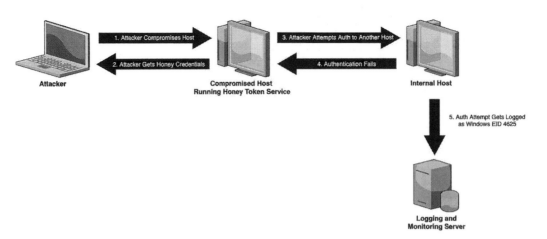

FIGURE 8-2:

Hiding Honey Credentials in LSA Secrets Reveals Attackers Attempting Privilege Escalation

 SEE: The goal is for the attacker to see the username and password tied to a service account when they dump LSA Secrets.

 THINK: The attacker should think these credentials provide elevated access to the system they're interacting with or others.

 DO: When the attacker attempts authentication to any Windows system using the credentials, we'll know they are on the network.

Configuring the Honeypot

While we'll supply an intentionally incorrect password for the honey token service, this technique does require a real username to work. So, you'll want to create one. Since nobody should log on to this account for a legitimate purpose, you can go ahead and set the account to disabled (Figure 8-3).

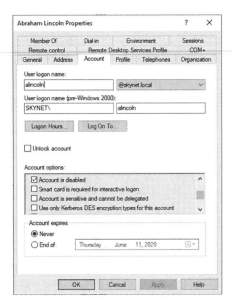

FIGURE 8-3:

The alincoln account is disabled, and only exists for this honey token service. We'll watch it closely.

Now it's time to create the service. On the endpoint that will host the service, run the following command:

```
sc create BackupSvc binPath="C:\Program Files\Symantec\Backup\backupsvc.
exe" obj="alincoln@skynet"¹ password="notgonnawork"
```

Let's break this command down:

- **sc create**: The sc program invokes the create function to create a new service.
- **BackupSvc**: This is the name of the service. It should be unique and appealing to an attacker.
- **binPath= "C:\Program Files\Symantec\Backup\backupsvc.exe"**: This path to the executable linked to the service. The path doesn't have to exist but should be related to the service name and seem believable and interesting.
- **obj= "alincoln@skynet"**: The username that would launch the service. It must be an actual username on your system or domain.
- **password= "notgonnawork":** The password that would authenticate the user launching the service. The trick here is that this should not be the real password for this account. The fake password should be somewhat complex and look like what an administrator might use for an actual service account password.

---

¹ If you're testing this on a workstation that isn't a domain member, you should use the format obj="hostname\username" instead of obj="username@domain"

If the command runs successfully, you should see a return message like this:

```
[SC] CreateService SUCCESS
```

The new service should show up in the services.msc console, as shown in Figure 8-4.

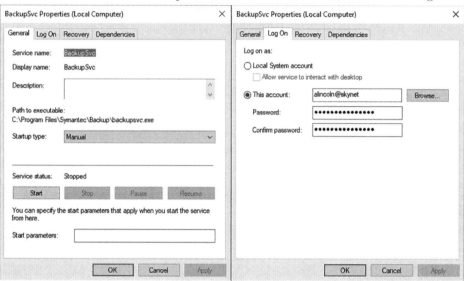

FIGURE 8-4:

The honey token service looks real to an attacker, but never actually runs

With the service present, any attacker dumping LSA secrets will likely stumble upon the clear text credentials associated with it. While that process is a bit beyond the scope of this book, there are several tools and techniques that'll lead them down the path of discovery (Figure 8-5).

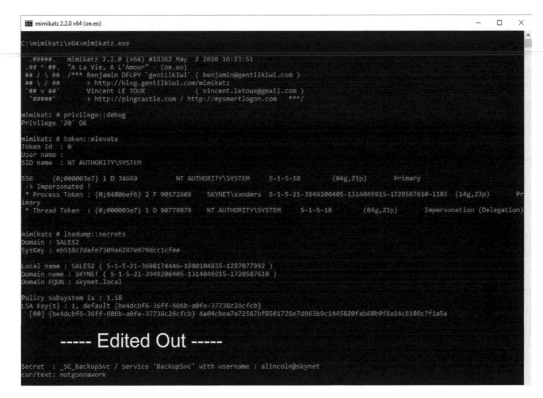

```
mimikatz 2.2.0 x64 (oe.eo)                                                      —   □   ×

C:\mimikatz\x64>mimikatz.exe

  .#####.   mimikatz 2.2.0 (x64) #18362 May  2 2020 16:23:51
 .## ^ ##.  "A La Vie, A L'Amour" - (oe.eo)
 ## / \ ##  /*** Benjamin DELPY `gentilkiwi` ( benjamin@gentilkiwi.com )
 ## \ / ##       > http://blog.gentilkiwi.com/mimikatz
 '## v ##'       Vincent LE TOUX             ( vincent.letoux@gmail.com )
  '#####'        > http://pingcastle.com / http://mysmartlogon.com   ***/

mimikatz # privilege::debug
Privilege '20' OK

mimikatz # token::elevate
Token Id  : 0
User name :
SID name  : NT AUTHORITY\SYSTEM

556     {0;000003e7} 1 D 34669      NT AUTHORITY\SYSTEM    S-1-5-18      (04g,21p)      Primary
 -> Impersonated !
 * Process Token : {0;0480bef6} 2 F 90572669    SKYNET\sanders  S-1-5-21-3949206405-1314046915-1728587610-1103  (14g,23p)      Pr
imary
 * Thread Token  : {0;000003e7} 1 D 90779879    NT AUTHORITY\SYSTEM    S-1-5-18      (04g,21p)      Impersonation (Delegation)

mimikatz # lsadump::secrets
Domain : SALES2
SysKey : eb518c7dafe7309a6287e979dcc1cfee

Local name : SALES2 ( S-1-5-21-3698174446-1980104835-1287077992 )
Domain name : SKYNET ( S-1-5-21-3949206405-1314046915-1728587610 )
Domain FQDN : skynet.local

Policy subsystem is : 1.18
LSA Key(s) : 1, default {be4dcbf6-36ff-686b-a0fe-37738c26cfcb}
  [00] {be4dcbf6-36ff-686b-a0fe-37738c26cfcb} 4a04cbea7e72567bf8561728e7d963b9c1445820fab60b0f8a14c6186c7f1a5a

 ----- Edited Out -----

Secret  : _SC_BackupSvc / service 'BackupSvc' with username : alincoln@skynet
cur/text: notgonnawork
```

FIGURE 8-5:

Dumping LSA secrets using Mimikatz[2] reveals the honey token service credentials

Discoverability

If you've set up the honey token service as I've described, there's not much else to do from the standpoint of ensuring the attacker discovers it once they've compromised that system. If they dump LSA secrets, they'll see the account, and they'll typically use it in some way. It helps if the account stands out in some form, perhaps having a name that identifies it as a service account. You can either include that in the account name itself like "svc_backp" or name the account after a real or common service name, like "solarwinds".

You should focus deployment around common footholds since that's where attackers are likely to gain initial access and start working towards furthering control and lateral movement. The more systems you deploy the service on, the more likely you are to catch an attacker. You might even consider building honey token services into the base "gold" images you build user workstations from.

---

[2] Mimikatz is a post-exploitation tool that allows dumping passwords from memory, pass-the-hash attacks, and other techniques facilitating lateral movement on Windows systems. Learn more about it at https://github.com/gentilkiwi/mimikatz.

Interactivity

With honey credentials, interactivity mostly pertains to whether you'll allow the credentials to provide access to any resource. You wouldn't do that in this scenario since you're giving fake credentials.

Monitoring

We'll rely on Windows logging to monitor for attackers using the honey credentials they've stolen. To do so, you should enable the appropriate logging facility.

For a system or group of systems hosting honey files in a Windows domain, follow these steps:

1. Access the **Group Policy Management** tool from the **Administrative Tools** folder on the Start Menu.
2. Browse to whatever policy manages your enterprise logging policy, right-click it, and select **Edit**.
3. Browse to **Computer Configuration > Policies > Windows Settings > Security Settings > Local Policies > Audit Policy.**
4. Double-click **Audit Logon Events.**
5. Place a checkmark next to **Define these policy settings** and **Failure**.
6. Click **OK** and close the policy editor.

This policy should apply organization-wide. Just because the attacker stole credentials from one machine doesn't mean they'll only attempt to use them on that system. With logon failure auditing enabled everywhere, you see anywhere they try to move to and gain a better understanding of their current vantage point.

Enabling logon failure auditing generates Security Event ID (EID) 4625 whenever the attacker attempts to log in to the honey account with the credentials we've supplied (Figure 8-6).

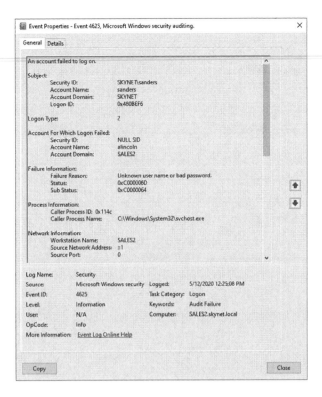

FIGURE 8-6:

Event ID 4625 indicates failed authentication using honey credentials tied to our fake service

Event ID: 4625

Provider: Microsoft-Windows-Security-Auditing.

Event Description: An account failed to log on.

Behavior: This event reports failed attempts to authenticate to a system, regardless of the logon type or whether the account is disabled.

Enablement: For this log to be generated, Audit Logon Events must be enabled, as described previously.

Investigative Details:

- **Logged/Timestamp**: When the attacker attempted authentication. Use this to plot a point on your investigation timeline.
- **Subject/Account** [SubjectUserName]: The name of the account reporting the logon failure.
- **Account for Which Logon Failed/Account Name** [TargetUserName]: The name of the honey account.

- **Logon Type** [LogonType]: The type of logon attempted[3]. It can indicate the attacker's level of access (interactive, command line, etc.).
- **Caller Process Name** [ProcessName]: The process that attempted the logon. It might indicate the level of access the attacker has or the tooling they're using.
- **Caller Process ID** [ProcessID]: The hexadecimal representation of the PID from the process that attempted the logon.
- **Network Information/Workstation Name** [WorkstationName]: The system where the logon occurred from.
- **Network Information/Source Network Address** [IpAddress]: The network location where the logon occurred from, if applicable.

This SIGMA rule alerts when someone attempts authentication with the stolen credentials:

```
title: Honey Token Service Credentials Used
description: Someone attempted to log in with credentials tied to a honey
token service.
date: 2020/01/01
tags:
    - honeypot
author: Chris Sanders
logsource:
    product: windows
    service: security
detection:
    selection:
        EventID: 4625
        TargetUserName: %HONEYCRED_USERNAME_HERE%
    condition: selection
fields:
    -   SubjectUserName
    -   TargetUserName
    -   TargetDomainName
    -   LogonType
    -   ProcessName
    -   ProcessId
    -   WorkstationName
    -   IpAddress
level: critical
```

---

[3] See a list of logon types here: https://docs.microsoft.com/en-us/windows/security/threat-protection/auditing/event-4625.

Since the honey token service has no legitimate function, there's no reason it should ever attempt to start. If someone does try to start it, it'll attempt to launch as the service user. The authentication attempt fails with the wrong password, so it also generates EID 4625. You'll know if that's what happened with the presence of System EID 7000, indicating the service failed to start due to a logon failure. This event might be the product of an errant user or sysadmin, but you'll want to investigate it all the same.

If you create multiple honey accounts with unique names and track their deployment in a spreadsheet or with some other mechanism, you'll have a better sense of where your attacker is and where they've been. At a high level, you can divide these accounts by region, site, or network segment. Better yet, deploying unique services per machine maximizes your ability to track what the attacker has compromised. This necessitates automation, so you'll want to look into scripting the creation of these users and services if your honey token service deployment grows significantly.

Honey Credentials in Memory

I've already shown you how you can take advantage of attackers dumping LSA secrets to gain credentials of privilege escalation or lateral movement. But, this is not the only manner in which you can leverage the Window Local Security Authority to get honey credentials in front of the adversary. Attackers also frequently attack the LSA Subsystem Service (LSASS), which is responsible for enforcing security policies on the system.

As part of LSASS's security enforcement, it often has to store passwords in memory in one form or another. The password might be in clear text or hashed form, depending on some system variables. While this information isn't accessible directly by users, attackers can use many techniques to dump LSASS process memory and extract passwords from that output. Even if they only end up with a password hash, the attacker might crack the hash offline to use it in a pass-the-hash[4] attack.

Knowing that attackers frequently look in LSASS's memory for credentials allows you to seed this location with your own honey credentials. Whenever an attacker attempts to use them, you'll know they've compromised a system somewhere on the network (Figure 8-7).

---

[4] Learn more about PtH attacks and mitigation strategies here: https://www.microsoft.com/en-us/download/details.aspx?id=36036.

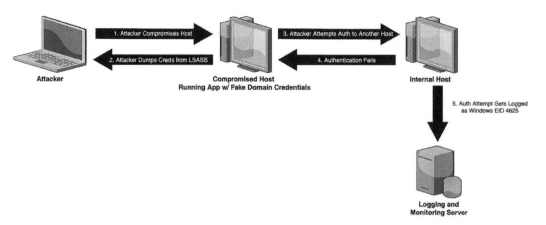

FIGURE 8-7:

When attackers dump credentials from LSASS, they'll find honey credentials

 SEE: The goal is for the attacker to see the username and password tied to the fake domain account when they dump LSASS.

 THINK: The attacker should think these credentials provide elevated access to the system they're interacting with or others.

 DO: When the attacker attempts authentication to any Windows system using the credentials, we'll know they are on the network.

Configuring the Honeypot

Inserting honey credentials into memory isn't too tricky. As a proof of concept, try this yourself by running the following command I learned from my friend Mark Baggett[5]:

```
runas /user:skynet\jcarter /netonly cmd.exe
```

After running the command, Windows prompts you to provide a password. The beauty of this sequence is that the user account jcarter doesn't exist in the domain, so the password you enter is irrelevant. Regardless, runas launches another command prompt under the context of whatever user account you used to execute the runas command, but any outbound connections use the non-existent skynet\jcarter account. That won't be too useful for much since that account doesn't have access to anything, but it does place the credentials for the account into LSASS. Figure 8-8 shows my use of the above command

---

[5] https://isc.sans.edu/diary/Detecting+Mimikatz+Use+On+Your+Network/19311

(1), creation of the second cmd.exe window (2), and using Mimikatz to dump the honey credentials from LSASS (3).

FIGURE 8-8:

Using runas with a fictional account inserts credentials into LSASS

While this demonstrates our goal, there is a limitation. Whenever you close the command prompt window, the credentials leave memory. If you leave these windows open on user machines, it's likely that they notice and close them and dash your honeypot dreams. As a workaround, you can use the New-HoneyHash Powershell script from Matt Graeber and the PowerShell Empire project to achieve the same result more covertly: https://github.com/EmpireProject/Empire/blob/dev/data/module_source/management/New-HoneyHash.ps1.

To make this work, download the script and add the following line to the bottom of the file:

```
New-HoneyHash -Domain skynet -Username jcarter -Password peanuts
```

This command invokes the function New-HoneyHash function with the parameters you define:

- -file: The location of New-HoneyHash.ps1
- -Domain: Your domain name.

- • -Username: The fake username identifying the honey credential.
- • -Password: A fake password that can be anything.

Now, you're ready to run the script, like this:

```
powershell -windowstyle hidden -noexit -file C:\New-HoneyHash.ps1
```

When executed, New-HoneyHash leaves Powershell running in the process tree thanks to the `-noexit` command line argument, but it's unlikely that this artifact draws the attention of the attacker. The `-windowstyle hidden` argument ensures there won't be any lingering windows that users are likely to close.

You can build this script into existing login scripts, set it as a scheduled task when users login to systems, or use whatever your preferred persistence mechanism might be. Since the script will hang around on the system, be sure to rename it to something that won't draw an attacker's attention.

Discoverability

Just like I've discussed with honey token services, if the credentials you've supplied are in LSASS, there's not much else for you to do. Focus honey credential placement on common footholds like end-user workstations or hosts in your DMZ. Attackers are sometimes careful about dumping LSASS on servers, as certain conditions can cause system crashes that defenders or users might notice. Still, placing these tokens in sensitive locations isn't a bad idea.

Interactivity

The credentials you'll use for honey credentials in memory aren't real, so they won't provide access to any network resources. Thus, there are no additional interactivity concerns.

Monitoring

Just like with honey token services, you'll monitor for Windows Event ID 4625 to find failed logins tied to the honey credentials you've created. Because the username and password doesn't exist, any attempt to login to a system or domain resource results in a failed login attempt that you should monitor and alert on.

Alerts from the use of these honey credentials are incredibly high fidelity, and you should treat them accordingly. Don't forget that users often reuse passwords, and attackers know this as well. This means attackers might attempt to use their stolen credentials on non-Windows services like internal web apps, VPN portals, and third-party tools. Where possible, build detection alerts from these log sources as well to better understand the attacker's goals.

As another response consideration, consider running Mimikatz yourself on hosts where you know attackers have already run it[6]. This output provides a list of other credentials that the attacker obtained. You'll use this information to prepare for the isolation of the incident and eradication of the attacker.

Honey Broadcasts

Attackers don't always have to aggressively seek out credentials to further their sphere of influence over a network. Sometimes, those credentials come to them if they patiently wait and listen. One such example of how attackers steal credentials involves leveraging the Windows Link Local Multicast Name Resolution (LLMNR) service.

LLMNR is a Windows component that assists in host identification, somewhat similar to DNS. When a host wants to resolve the IP address of a hostname, it can utilize LLMNR to send multicast packets to all other hosts on the same network. Ideally, the host with the IP address responds. Communication begins once the sending host has the hostname to IP address mapping. I've depicted a simplified version of this process in Figure 8-9.

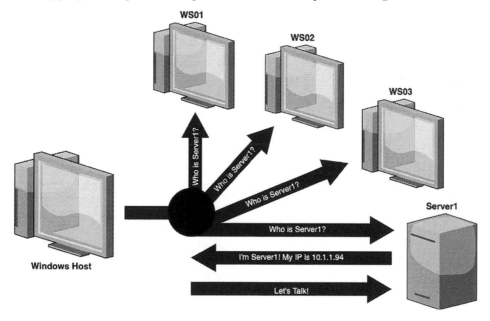

FIGURE 8-9:

LLMNR provides a mechanism for IP to hostname mapping on Window systems. Ideally, only the host with the hostname requested responds.

---

[6] Of course, this might let attackers know you're there. You'll have to weigh that risk with the reward of more efficient response.

Think of this as someone standing in a room and yelling, "Where's Chris?!" Everyone hears it, but since I'm the only Chris there, I respond by saying, "Chris Sanders, that's me!" Now that person and I can communicate. But what if someone else not named Chris responded faster and louder than I did?

Like many other protocols that rely on broadcast type messages, attackers can take advantage. Look at the example I've laid out in Figure 8-10. Here, WS05 sends an LLMNR packet to everyone on the network that says, "Who is Server1?" Ideally, Server1 responds with its IP address. But, there's nothing stopping an attacker on an entirely different host they control from responding first. That's what happens from the attacker controlled WS03 system. WS03 says, "I'm Server1, and my IP address is 10.1.1.24!" Now, WS05 attempts to communicate with WS03 as though it is Server1. At this point, if WS05 attempts an action that requires authentication, it sends the initiating user's username and NTLMv2 password hash to the attacker's system. Now, the attacker can either use the hash in a pass-the-hash attack to impersonate the legitimate user or crack the password offline to get the clear text version. Practitioners refer to this technique as LLMNR Poisoning.

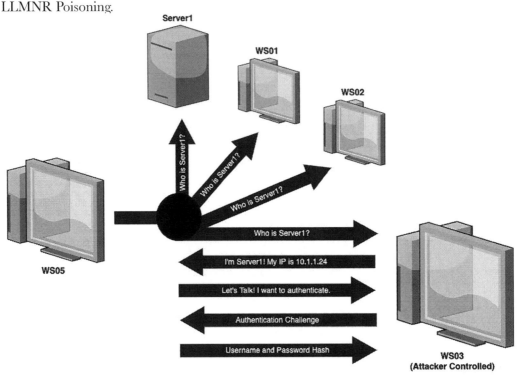

FIGURE 8-10:

The attacker-controlled WS03 responds as though it were Server1, allowing it to challenge for credentials and harvest password hashes

Now that you know how attackers take advantage of this protocol, let's consider how we can flip the attack around on them. If attackers on your network are waiting for LLMNR packets, let's give them some! We'll use a dedicated system to effectively create a honey broadcast that lures attackers to respond so that we can transmit honey credentials to them. We'll monitor for anyone using those credentials to alert us to the attacker's presence (Figure 8-11).

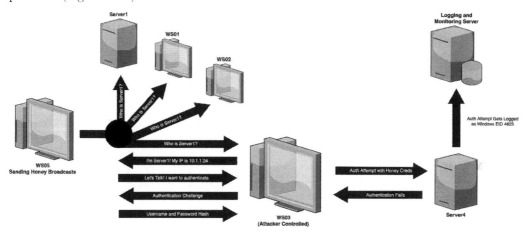

FIGURE 8-11:

We'll use honey broadcasts to lure in attackers and give them honey credentials. We'll monitor for the use of those credentials all over the network.

 SEE: The goal is for the attacker to see the LLMNR requests we're broadcasting over a network segment.

 THINK: The attacker should think this broadcast is a legitimate LLMNR request from a host seeking a hostname-to-IP mapping.

 DO: When the attacker responds to the fake LLMNR broadcast, we'll initiate authentication to their system with honey credentials. When they attempt authentication to any Windows system using the credentials, we'll know they are on the network.

Configuring the Honeypot

Creating an LLMNR broadcast is reasonably straightforward. Assuming LLMNR isn't disabled[7] on your host, open Windows Explorer and type **hostname** for a host that

---

[7] Because LLMNR poisoning can be such an effective attack, most security practitioners recommend disabling the service, as discussed here: https://www.blackhillsinfosec.com/how-to-disable-llmnr-why-you-want-to/. You can still disable LLMNR network wide and leave it enabled for a single host per network segment to facilitate this honeypot.

doesn't exist on your network. You won't see any visual indication it's happening, but a packet sniffer like Wireshark reveals the transmission of LLMNR packets attempting hostname resolution (Figure 8-12).

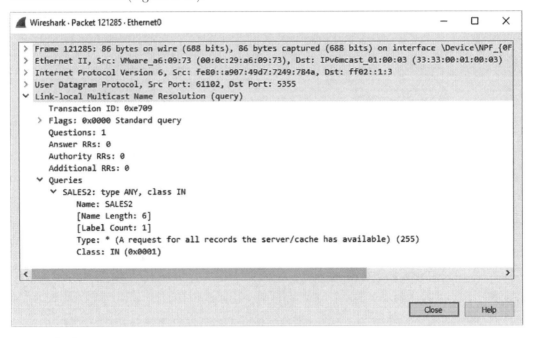

FIGURE 8-12:

LLMNR packets seeking a host-to-IP mapping for SALES2

There are a few ways an attacker might intercept and respond to this request to obtain credentials, but one of the easiest is running Responder[8], a Python script that facilitates various types of network protocol poisoning. Responder automatically intercepts and poisons LLMNR broadcasts to obtain password hashes (Figure 8-13).

---

[8] Learn more about Responder at https://github.com/lgandx/Responder.

FIGURE 8-13:

Responder intercepts a username and password hash through automatic LLMNR poisoning

This example demonstrates how LLMNR poisoning works, but it also exposes legitimate network credentials, which isn't something we want. It also isn't scalable, since you can't sit at a terminal continually trying to browse to non-existent hosts 24 hours a day[9]. To make this more efficient, we'll use the Invoke-HoneyCreds-IDH.ps1 PowerShell script below to automate the creation of LLMNR broadcasts with fake credentials[10].

```
# LLMNR Honey Broadcast Generator
# Adapted from Ben0xa - https://github.com/Ben0xA/PowerShellDefense/blob/
master/Invoke-HoneyCreds.ps1
# Provide honey credentials at the bottom.

function Invoke-HoneyCreds {
    [CmdletBinding()]
  Param (
      [Parameter(Mandatory = $True, Position = 0)]
      [ValidateNotNullOrEmpty()]
```

---

[9] Or maybe you can. How you utilize your interns is none of my business.

[10] You can download this script from https://github.com/chrissanders/idh.

```
        [String]
        $domain,

        [Parameter(Mandatory = $True, Position = 1)]
        [ValidateNotNullOrEmpty()]
        [String]
        $user,

        [Parameter(Mandatory = $True, Position = 1)]
        [ValidateNotNullOrEmpty()]
        [String]
        $password
    )

    # Add Member Defition for LogonUser
    $api = Add-Type -Name Ignore -MemberDefinition @"
        [DllImport("advapi32.dll", SetLastError = true)]
        public static extern bool LogonUser(string lpszUsername,
string lpszDomain, string lpszPassword, int dwLogonType, int
dwLogonProvider, ref IntPtr phToken);
"@ -passthru

    $securepass = ConvertTo-SecureString "$password" -AsPlainText
-Force
    $creds = New-Object System.Management.Automation.PSCredential
-ArgumentList ($user, $securepass)

    $plain = "$($user):$($password)"

    # Impersonate the new user
    [IntPtr]$token = [Security.Principal.
WindowsIdentity]::GetCurrent().Token
    $api::LogonUser($user, $domain, $password, 9, 0, [ref]$token) |
Out-Null
    $identity = New-Object Security.Principal.WindowsIdentity $token
    $context = $Identity.Impersonate()


    while($True) {
        try {
            New-PSDrive -name X -PSProvider FileSystem -root
\\$($domain)\C$ -Credential $creds -ErrorAction Ignore -ErrorVariable
$err

        }
        catch {

        }
```

```
            Start-Sleep -s 5
    }
}

# Provide credentials here. The domain and username should be real, but
the password should be fake.

Invoke-HoneyCreds -domain skynet -user jcarter -password peanuts
```

You should save the script to whatever system will generate the honey broadcasts and modify the variables at the bottom of the script to reflect your real domain name and whatever fake honey credentials you wish to use. From there, simply execute the script. It attempts to map a network drive to a non-existent resource every 5 seconds, resulting in LLMNR broadcasts. An attacker listening on a host they've already compromised with a tool like Responder should intercept these requests and be rewarded with the honey credentials (Figure 8-14).

FIGURE 8-14:

Running Invoke-HoneyCreds-IDH.ps1 (top) sends honey broadcasts (middle), resulting in the attacker eventually obtaining honey credentials (bottom)

Discoverability

LLMNR broadcasts leverage multicast transmission at the link layer, meaning any attacker on the same local network broadcast domain should see the honey broadcast[11].

---

[11] Check out this video for a brief description of broadcast domains: https://www.youtube.com/watch?v=pX2OsymkeVU.

As such, you should deploy honey broadcast nodes across each of the segments on your network to take full advantage of this technique. Focus on segments composed of common footholds and sensitive assets.

Interactivity

The attacker should easily derive NTLMv2 hashes from their successful LLMNR attack. That provides some level of interactivity, as they can now attempt pass-the-hash techniques to impersonate that user. This move won't work since the user isn't valid, but that's fine because Windows logs the attempt all the same.

Something to ponder, however, is that the attack surface exposed to pass-the-hash techniques is smaller than if the attacker had a clear text password. With the former, they must use specialized tools and can only authenticate in a limited number of ways. For the latter, they can simply enter the password into authentication prompts as they move through the network. Not only that, but they can also try the password on non-Windows infrastructure, such as internal web apps. Users reuse passwords, and attackers know this.

While the credentials you'll give to the attacker are fake, I recommend making the password something that is easily crackable with basic dictionary attacks (Shown in Figure 8-15)[12]. That way, it lowers the time cost for the attacker to use the honey credentials, increasing their potential opportunity for interaction and your chance to catch them.

```
sanders@idh1:~$ ./john-1.9.0-jumbo-1/run/john --format=netntlmv2 hash.txt
Using default input encoding: UTF-8
Loaded 1 password hash (netntlmv2, NTLMv2 C/R [MD4 HMAC-MD5 32/64])
Warning: OpenMP is disabled; a non-OpenMP build may be faster
Proceeding with single, rules:Single
Press 'q' or Ctrl-C to abort, almost any other key for status
Warning: Only 7 candidates buffered for the current salt, minimum 8 needed for performance.
Warning: Only 5 candidates buffered for the current salt, minimum 8 needed for performance.
Warning: Only 4 candidates buffered for the current salt, minimum 8 needed for performance.
Almost done: Processing the remaining buffered candidate passwords, if any.
Proceeding with wordlist:./john-1.9.0-jumbo-1/run/password.lst, rules:Wordlist
peanuts          (jcarter)
1g 0:00:00:00 DONE 2/3 (2020-05-15 16:07) 11.11g/s 76844p/s 76844c/s 76844C/s partner..precious
Use the "--show --format=netntlmv2" options to display all of the cracked passwords reliably
Session completed
```

FIGURE 8-15:

An attacker might use a tool like John the Ripper to crack the password hash

Monitoring

Monitoring for credential use here looks the same as the other examples I described

---

[12] While it's incredibly tempting, I suggest avoiding passwords that purposely taunt the attacker, like 'tryharder' or 'comeatmebro.'

in this chapter. Assuming you use fake credentials, the attacker should cause failed authentications resulting in Event ID 4625.

EID 4625 tells you where the attacker attempted to use the credentials. Because honey broadcasts are limited to the broadcast domain, this means you'll likely deploy several broadcasters across your network. You should use individual accounts for each segment; that way, you know where the attacker has been as well. Keep track of where you're using each account in a spreadsheet to quickly scope attackers when honey broadcast alerts fire.

> ## FROM THE TRENCHES:
>
> While I've instructed you to create dedicated fake accounts for most honey credentials in this chapter, a colleague once came up with another useful strategy. Whenever an employee left the organization, rather than deleting their account, they changed the password and used them as deception objects. The accounts already look real, and this has the added benefit of potentially detecting former employees attempting to reach data they are no longer authorized to access. Just remember to disable the accounts or limit their logon hours to never to allow authentication.

More Honey Credentials

There are far too many ways to lure attackers toward interaction with honey credentials than I can cover in this book. Now that you understand the concept, you can use the examples I've provided as a launch point to explore other ideas that expose attackers to credentials of many types from multiple sources. More honey credential strategies might include:

- **SSH Honey Keys**: Some attackers make it a point to search compromised systems for SSH keys that help them move laterally since those are often more ubiquitous than passwords. Leave invalid SSH keys in places they're likely to be discovered, and monitor for authentication attempts to your SSH-enabled hosts.
- **AWS IAM Credentials**: Attackers increasingly target cloud-hosted assets as more organizations move infrastructure to outside the traditional perimeter. Take advantage by creating an AWS IAM credential with no explicit permissions and leave it in places where attackers might discover it. Then, set up CloudTrail and CloudWatch to notify when someone uses the

credential to attempt authentication. Learn more about this technique here: https://blog.rapid7.com/2016/11/30/early-warning-detectors-using-aws-access-keys-honeytokens/. For a more turnkey solution, you can also check out Atlassian's SpaceCrab project at https://bitbucket.org/asecurityteam/spacecrab/.

- **Honey Tables**: Attackers frequently target web servers looking for SQL injection or other vulnerabilities that could grant them access to the back-end database supporting the site. Once there, they execute queries to find and dump the users table in hopes they'll discover credentials that can elevate their privilege or that they can use elsewhere. With this in mind, rename your actual users table something less obvious and create a users honey table full of honey credentials. Monitor for authentication attempts with these credentials on the web app, and other locations on your network.

- **WPAD Honey Broadcasts**: The same principle I showed you for using honey broadcasts to share honey credentials with attackers works for other broadcast-based protocols. For example, Windows systems use the Web Proxy Auto-Discovery Protocol (WPAD) to find proxy servers so users can browse over the internet. An attacker who intercepts one of these broadcasts can respond with a configuration file allowing them to serve as a proxy for that host. This sequence results in a man-in-the-middle attack where the attacker's system intercepts the victim's internet traffic. You can take advantage of the attacker by sending WPAD honey broadcasts from a dedicated honeypot host. Once the attacker starts proxying the friendly hosts browsing, the honeypot host sends authentication requests to an externally hosted server. The attacker intercepts these credentials and attempts to use them, but they don't work. At the same time, you're monitoring that external host, which you own, for the authentication attempt.

Conclusion

Much of deception-based detection is giving attackers what they think they want, and attackers often want network or service credentials more than most other things. In this chapter, I described several methods for providing attackers with honey credentials that appear real, but ultimately lure them into carefully monitored traps. By using techniques like honey token services, honey credentials in memory, and honey broadcasts, you leverage knowledge about common attacks to provide high-efficacy detection.

UNCONVENTIONAL HONEYPOTS

EVERY HONEYPOT I'VE DISCUSSED SO FAR FITS NEATLY into the categories of honey system, service, or token. While I've done my best to classify most honeypots within the constructs of these easily identifiable types, not every honeypot fits those molds perfectly. In this final chapter, I want to show you some honeypots that are a bit hard to classify. Along with this, I'll also show you honeypots that are useful for detecting more unique forms of attacker activity and honeypots that are simply more creative extensions of previously demonstrated concepts. We'll look at DHCP honey services, honey tokens for detecting cloned websites, SQL honey tables, honey mailboxes, and honey commands.

DHCP Honey Service

If you've ever spent time administering a network, then you've probably benefited from DHCP at some point. The Dynamic Host Configuration Protocol (DHCP) handles automatic addressing of network clients so you don't have to. If a system wants to communicate on the network but doesn't have an IP address, it requests one from the DHCP server. The server provides the address, and communication commences (Figure 9-1).

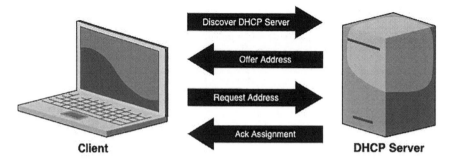

FIGURE 9-1:

DHCP servers provide IP addresses to hosts that ask

However, not everyone uses DHCP all the time. Many administrators explicitly avoid it on secure networks. This decision is common in segments containing servers, industrial control systems, and non-computer network devices like VoIP phones and printers. The theory is that the things on these network segments are tightly controlled. Anything that gets added to them goes through well-defined change management processes, so you don't want something to communicate on the network that isn't supposed to be there. By avoiding DHCP, an attacker that plugs into the network or tries to create a new network interface on a system must assign an address manually. This scenario would be hard to detect if the attacker doesn't cross a network sensor boundary where you can look for non-approved addresses.

Avoiding DHCP on sensitive segments like these makes sense. But this is where we'll take a detour from that conventional approach and apply a deception-based detection technique to the problem. If every device on the network segment has a manually assigned IP address, then it would be anomalous if someone tried to request one from a DHCP server. So, we'll set up a DHCP server with the sole purpose of logging IP address request interaction. When this happens, we'll know there's an attacker on the network or somebody misconfigured something (Figure 9-2). This strategy provides a simple mechanism for detecting physical breaches in secured areas.

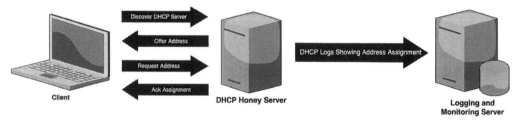

FIGURE 9-2:

A DHCP honey service responds to addressing requests from hosts on segments where these requests shouldn't be made

SEE: The goal is for the attacker to see a high-value network segment.

 THINK: The attacker should think the network segment contains targets relevant to their goals.

 DO: When the attacker attempts to obtain an IP address on the network segment, a DHCP request lets us know they're there.

Configuring the Honeypot

The first step for this honeypot is configuring the DHCP server service. There are several tools available for this task, but you won't need any fancy bells and whistles. To demonstrate a proof of concept, I'll show you how to set up a honeypot using the ISC DHCP service on Ubuntu Linux. Before completing these steps, be sure that no other DHCP servers operate within the segment you're targeting[1]. Failure to do this could make DHCP servers compete for addresses and knock production systems offline.

First, install the DHCP server service:

```
sudo apt-get install isc-dhcp-server
```

Next, set the network interface through which the service will respond to requests. Edit **/etc/default/isc-dhcp-server** and type the network interface next to the **INTERFACESv4** setting, like this:

```
# On what interfaces should the DHCP server (dhcpd) serve DHCP requests?
#      Separate multiple interfaces with spaces, e.g. "eth0 eth1".
INTERFACESv4="ens33"
```

Now, configure the DHCP service settings in **/etc/dhcp/dhcpd.conf**. This file is where you'll define what IP address information is handed out by the service. Below, I define the subnet 10.100.50.0/24 and an available range of 10.100.50.1-254. You can just add this to the top of the configuration file. The subnet range here should match the subnet bound to the network interface you're using.

---

[1] If you're doing this in a lab, consider using a virtual machine on a dedicated virtual network. As a rule, don't deploy DHCP servers on a network unless you're authorized to do so and fully understand the ramifications of your action.

```
subnet 10.100.50.0 netmask 255.255.255.0 {
  range 10.100.50.1 10.100.50.254;
}
```

Finally, within the same file, uncomment the following line by removing the pound sign to designate this DHCP server as authoritative for the network segment:

```
#authoritative;
```

After saving and closing the file, you're ready to start the DHCP service[2].

```
sudo systemctl start isc-dhcp-server.service
```

Now, any device on the same network segment as the DHCP server without an IP address should request and receive one from the DHCP honey service. When that happens, you'll know that you have an unauthorized (or misconfigured) network interface communicating on this network. If you'd like to test this, configure a host on the same network as the honey service to obtain an IP address automatically. If it gets one from the range specified in the DHCP service configuration, you'll know everything is working.

Discoverability

For the most part, you'll rely on attackers finding their way to sensitive network segments containing DHCP honey services on their own. The attacker's natural movement from common footholds towards their goals likely pulls them in the direction of servers and other sensitive assets. I wouldn't recommend taking any special actions to push them in that direction since you don't want to actively help them.

For the DHCP honey service itself, keep in mind that DHCP works using broadcast packets. Clients that need IP addresses don't know where the DHCP server is, so they send out DHCP Discover packets to every system in the network broadcast domain. The DHCP server responds with an Offer packet. Now that the client knows where the server is, they can complete the transaction with Request and Acknowledgement packets. The coverage of the DHCP honey service only extends as far as the network broadcast domain you place it in. This limitation means you may have to deploy multiple DHCP servers to different network segments.

Interactivity

Exposing the DHCP service to the network segment allows an attacker to discover and

---

[2] If you want the service to persist by automatically starting on boot, also run sudo systemctl enable isc-dhcp-server.service.

request an IP address from it. However, just because you give the attacker an IP address doesn't mean you should give them a valid one, or even all the addressing information they want. Doing so would allow them to communicate on the network. We don't want that; we just want to know they're on the network. Assigning any IP address and logging it gets us there. So, you're best off issuing dark space IP addresses from the DHCP honey service. That is, an IP address that places the requesting host on its own network range, absent of any production systems. The attacker is likely to figure this out and assign their own address at some point, but it's useful to slow them down and cause a little confusion along the way.

In the example configuration above, the 10.100.50.0/24 network range is one such darknet. No production systems exist on that network, just the DHCP server interface. I also don't provide additional addresses you might expect to see in a DHCP response, like DNS servers and default gateways. Withholding this information limits the attacker's access and confuses them further, until such a point when they abandon the automatically assigned address for their own.

Monitoring

While you can detect and alert on DHCP transactions using network IDS, it's unlikely that all of this communication crosses a sensor boundary in common monitoring deployments. Therefore, you'll get more relevant data by monitoring DHCP service logs. ISC stores those logs in **/var/log/syslog** by default. The complete request and allocation of an IP address from the server to a potential attacker looks like this:

```
May 26 19:26:38 idh dhcpd[2882]: DHCPDISCOVER from 00:0c:29:e0:f6:f9 via
ens33
May 26 19:26:39 idh dhcpd[2882]: DHCPOFFER on 10.100.50.2 to
00:0c:29:e0:f6:f9 (client7) via ens33
May 26 19:26:39 idh dhcpd[2882]: DHCPREQUEST for 10.100.50.2
(10.100.50.1) from 00:0c:29:e0:f6:f9 (client7) via ens33
May 26 19:26:39 idh dhcpd[2882]: DHCPACK on 10.100.50.2 to
00:0c:29:e0:f6:f9 (client7) via ens33
```

This sequence of four log entries corresponds to the DHCP Discover-Offer-Request-Acknowledge (DORA) process. Once completed, the DHCP honey service allocates **10.100.50.2** to the attacker, who's communicating from the MAC address **00:0c:29:e0:f6:f9**.

This SIGMA rule alerts on the DHCP ACK data above. Although you could theoretically use any of the DHCP events, this entry indicates the IP address acquisition was successful and the attacker may start communicating with the assigned IP address[3].

```
title: DHCP Honey Service ACK
description: A DHCP honey service offered an IP address to a network
client on a segment where all hosts are statically assigned addresses.
date: 2020/01/01
tags:
    - honeypot
author: Chris Sanders
logsource:
    product: honeypot
    service: dhcp
detection:
    selection:
        type: DHCPACK
    condition: selection
fields:
    -  "Source MAC"
    -  "Client IP"
falsepositives:
    - Misconfigurations
level: high
```

You won't get a lot of data from this alert since the log is sparse, but you'll have enough to begin tracking down the source. This data includes:

- **Source MAC**: The MAC address of the attacker system. You can use this to track the communication down to a physical switch port or access point. The OUI of the MAC address (the first six bytes) might also provide clues to the type of device used, as it indicates the manufacturer[4].
- **Client IP**: The IP address assigned to the attacker's system. You'll use this to track any network activity they conduct.

In some cases, you might also encounter a sequence of logs that look like this:

```
May 26 19:26:35 idh dhcpd[2882]: DHCPREQUEST for 172.16.231.130 from
00:0c:29:e0:f6:f9 via ens33: wrong network.
May 26 19:26:35 idh dhcpd[2882]: DHCPNAK on 172.16.231.130 to
00:0c:29:e0:f6:f9 via ens33
```

A system that already has an IP address may request the same address again.

---

[3] Realistically, not every interface that communicates with a DHCP server actually accepts a request. Therefore, you might also consider alerting on DHCPDISCOVER logs, although they contain less information. Regardless, you'll want to record all these logs for the resulting investigation.

[4] Search the OUI database here: https://www.wireshark.org/tools/oui-lookup.html.

However, if it is on a new network, then the DHCP server responsible for that segment can tell it that it's on the wrong network and that the client must request a new address. That's what's happening here. The attacker came from a network segment where they had an address of 172.16.231.130, but that isn't valid on the new network for which this DHCP server is authoritative. So, it sends a DHCPNAK packet to the client. Now the client must request a new IP address using the process we've already looked at. These logs are useful because they provide the attacker's prior IP address. If this is a case of an attacker that moved an interface between networks (either physically or virtually), you'll now know where they came from and can investigate the events leading up to your alert.

A DHCP honey service provides a useful way to use a tool even when you don't actually want the service it offers. By deploying one in a zone where automatic addressing is prohibited, you gain the ability to detect attackers that stand-up new network interfaces in high-value areas. While I've demonstrated a proof of concept here, you'll want to ensure your implementation of the DHCP service is appropriately secured so that it doesn't become a target.

Cloned Website Honey Tokens

Nearly every major attack you read about, no matter how sophisticated, often has a human component. In many cases, attackers seeking to compromise your network leverage phishing attacks to lure users into clicking on malicious links or opening exploit-laden attachments. Phishing also provides an avenue for credential harvesting (Figure 9-3).

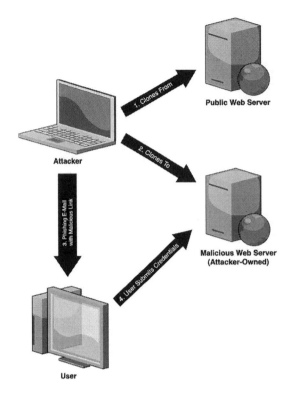

FIGURE 9-3:

Attackers clone legitimate websites to support credential harvesting

In a common form of credential harvesting, an attacker clones the content of a legitimate website that allows users to log in with a username and passwords. They host the cloned site on their own infrastructure and configure it to record submitted credentials. Then they send emails to users attempting to trick them into clicking a link to their cloned website and logging in to it. For example, they may claim that there has been a fraudulent charge on a bank account that the user needs to dispute, or that the user must log in and change their password or risk having an account purged. When the user supplies credentials to the cloned website, the attacker gets them and can now access that user's account.

Attackers that conduct credential harvesting attacks often clone banking or social media websites for broadly targeted attacks. However, attackers with more specific targets in mind may clone parts of your web infrastructure and target your users with their phishing emails. This action might be hard to detect through traditional mechanisms, but this is another case where you can use detection honeypots to your advantage.

In this example, I'll show you how to insert honey tokens into legitimate websites. When someone clones the site, a unique type of web bug notifies you (Figure 9-4).

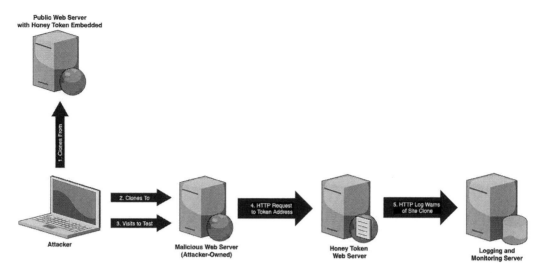

FIGURE 9-4:

Embedding a token in websites allows you to monitor for website cloning

 SEE: The goal is for the attacker to see a legitimate organization website.

 THINK: The attacker should think the website is benign, serving no other purpose than what it advertises.

 DO: When the attacker clones the website, we'll know they're planning something nefarious.

Configuring the Honeypot

For this honeypot, you'll start by identifying a web server on your network hosting an authentication page that an attacker might try to clone. Then, embed the following code[5] into the page somewhere:

```
<script>
if (document.domain != "chrissanders.org") {
    var l = location.href;
    var r = document.referrer;
    new Image().src = "http://%WEBSERVER%/pjt9887?l="+
            encodeURI(l) + "&amp;r=" + encodeURI(r);
}
```

[5] This code is adapted from the fine folks at Thinkst. Their CanaryToken tool can generate custom versions of it on-demand: https://github.com/thinkst/canarytokens.

```
</script>
```

Whenever someone visits the webpage, the JavaScript checks to see if the domain is actually where you're hosting the site (**chrissanders.org**). If the domain is anything else, as it would be in a cloned website scenario, the browser requests the honeypot web server domain (**%WEBSERVER%**), a unique token in the URL (**pjt9887**), the URL initially requested by the browser (**var l**), and the referring URL in the request (**var r**).

You'll need a functional web server to receive this connection request. Since the cloned website is most likely to be hosted outside your network, this web server should be accessible from the internet. If you'd like to try this yourself, follow the same web server setup instructions I provided in the Honeydocs section of Chapter 7.

Discoverability

For credential harvesting, attackers are most likely to clone externally facing websites that provide authentication. That might include web services tied to your core business function, web-based VPN portals, or externally facing employee tools like sales portals and benefits management. Assessing the web services you expose to the internet will help you determine what the most likely targets are. These are the locations you should place the honey token. There's not much special you should need to do to get attackers to notice these pages. After all, they're already valuable and fit with a specific goal the attacker has in mind.

While the web sites that attackers clone are visible, we'd prefer if our honey tokens weren't. When the attacker clones a website, the token will be there in plain sight if they go looking. Fortunately, attackers don't often examine these pages too carefully beyond modifying the form input variables to record passwords or adding in other malicious code of their own. In some cases, they've automated this process entirely[6].

If you are concerned about an attacker noticing the honey token code, a simple but effective strategy is to make sure that where you add the code segment has some visual distance between it and the authentication form inputs. The attacker is likely to notice the token code if it's right next to the form input, but those odds go down if they have to scroll to find it. If you want to go a bit farther, consider using a common attacker technique and obfuscating the JavaScript so its purpose is unclear. The attacker might not notice it at all now, or if they do, they may think you've already been attacked by someone else, laugh, and move on. There are tradeoffs to this approach, as some forms of

---

[6] If you'd like to test this out, Dave Kennedy's Social Engineering Toolkit (SET) had a feature to automatically clone a website, replace the form input variables, and host the new content. Learn more about SET at https://github.com/trustedsec/social-engineer-toolkit.

obfuscation might look more evident than the token code itself.

Interactivity

This simple honey token provides no interactivity that we want the attacker to be aware of. Because you're already inserting JavaScript into the page, you might be tempted to expand the code to do more profiling of the systems visiting the cloned page. Be wary of this, however. First, it provides more opportunity for the attacker to discover and remove your honey token code. Second, whatever code you insert will run in victims' browsers. That might have unintended adverse consequences.

Monitoring

Whenever someone browses to the cloned website while it's hosted at a domain other than the one it's supposed to be hosted on, the requester's browser invokes the honey token code. This action generates an HTTP request to the web server set up specifically to receive the request data. You'll monitor the web server access logs to generate alerts when this happens. Here's an example of one of those log entries from Apache:

```
198.51.100.22 - - [26/May/2020:17:12:16 +0000] "GET /pjt9887?l=http://
chrissanders.notreal270.org/&amp;r= HTTP/1.1" 404 491 "http://
chrissanders.notreal270.org/" "Mozilla/5.0 (Macintosh; Intel Mac OS X
10_15_4) AppleWebKit/537.36 (KHTML, like Gecko) Chrome/81.0.4044.138
Safari/537.36"
```

There are several useful pieces of information here:
- Timestamp (**26/May/2020:17:12:16 +0000**): When someone requested the cloned page. Use this to plot a point on your investigation timeline.
- Source IP Address (**198.51.100.22**): The IP address of the system that requested the cloned page. This address is likely either the attacker's victim or the attacker testing their tools.
- User Agent (**Mozilla/5.0 (Macintosh; Intel Mac OS X 10_15_4) AppleWebKit/537.36 (KHTML, like Gecko) Chrome/81.0.4044.138 Safari/537.36**): The user agent string provided by the application that requested the cloned page.
- HTTP Request: This contains information from the request itself and information the javascript added in the URL:
  - The domain where the attacker is hosting the cloned site (**chrissanders. notreal270.org**)
  - The honey token embedded in the page that was cloned (**pjt9887**)

- The original request made to the cloned page (**http://chrissanders. notreal270.org/**)
- The referrer in the original page request (blank in this case).

You should pair this log entry with detection rules to alert analysts when someone accesses a cloned version of a legitimate site. Here's a SIGMA rule that alerts on a log like the one above:

```
title: Cloned Website Visit
description: Someone cloned an internal website and is hosting it
elsewhere. This alert fires when someone visits the cloned site.
date: 2020/01/01
tags:
    - honeypot
author: Chris Sanders
logsource:
    product: honeytoken
    service: cloned_site
detection:
    selection:
        request_line|contains:
            - 'token1'
            - 'token2'
            - 'token3'
    condition: selection
fields:
    -   "Source IP"
    -   "User Agent"
    -   "HTTP Request"
falsepositives:
    - Chrome Lite⁷
level: high
```

Remember, this doesn't detect when an attacker clones the page. It detects when someone visits the cloned page. That could be one of the attacker's victims, but it could also be the attacker testing the functionality of their tooling. It might be hard to tell the difference between the two, but you can try by correlating the IP address of the honey token log with access logs in the legitimate version of the cloned website. Beyond that, the first request is more likely to be the attacker.

In either case, the person visiting the cloned site might not be one of your users, and the content almost certainly won't be hosted on your infrastructure. All the same, you don't want miscreants using your digital presence to commit crimes. Your best course of

---

⁷ Read more about this potential false positive here: https://blog.thinkst.com/2019/06/when-doc-umentdomain-is-not-equal-to.html.

action here is ensuring nobody on your network can access the cloned site while working with ISP and blocklist services to shut down or limit the broader world's ability to access the site[8]. The good news is that, using this technique, you'll be well equipped to start this process quickly. Perhaps even before the attacker has a chance to victimize anyone.

Honey Tables

Attackers often target databases because they hold sensitive information about an organization's customers or users. Not only that, but SQL injection vulnerabilities are also common in web applications, providing an attack surface that exposes databases if the attacker succeeds. In Chapter 8, I described how placing honey credentials in decoy tables was a useful technique for ensuring attackers discover those credentials when they compromise a database. However, we can go a bit farther to layer deception methods, which is what I'll show you here.

In this case, we want to know before an attacker attempts to use honey credentials they stole from a database. We'll create a honey table whose sole purpose is to entice interaction from the attacker so we'll know they're there. In this scenario, we'll assume the most common manifestation of this attack where the adversary accesses a database in an undesirable way through a web server.

 SEE: The goal is for the attacker to see an enticingly named database table.

 THINK: The attacker should think the table contains information useful to their goals.

 DO: When the attacker queries the table, we'll know they've gained an unacceptable level of access to the database server.

Configuring the Honeypot

Creating the honey table is relatively trivial. You should start with a functioning SQL server[9]. In this case, I'm running MySQL and I'm using a database called appdb. This database supports an e-commerce web application and is a real production database. To

---

[8] There are many of these sites, but consider starting with Google SafeBrowsing and Microsoft Security Intelligence.

[9] If you just want to experiment with this concept, this article will get you up and going with MySQL: https://www.digitalocean.com/community/tutorials/how-to-install-mysql-on-ubuntu-18-04.

create the honey table, I'll complete these steps:

1. Create a file containing fake user data. This table is a great place to place honey credentials, as I mentioned in Chapter 8. Here, I created a file named *db_users* and added this tab-delimited content[10]:

```
admin   gotcha
sanders         gotcha_again
jcalipari       allidoiswin
coachk  wishesiwerecoachcal
```

2. Log in to the MySQL server shell

```
sudo mysql -u username -p
```

3. Switch to the appdb database

```
use appdb;
```

4. Create the table. I'm using a simple, enticing name. The real user data is stored in another table.

```
CREATE TABLE company_users (username varchar(20), password
varchar(50));
```

5. Insert the users' data from the file into the table

```
LOAD DATA LOCAL INFILE 'db_users' INTO TABLE company_users;
```

With the honey table in the database, an attacker that gains access to the database is likely to find it when they enumerate the tables. Most attackers won't be able to resist taking a peek at the data.

Discoverability

When attackers eventually gain access to a database, their next action typically depends on their level of interactivity and expertise. Some attackers attempt to enumerate tables names based on characteristics of the web app itself, while others search for commonly named tables. You can take advantage of either to ensure the attacker finds your honey table.

You'll likely find the most success naming your table after things attacker's desire. For example, **users** or **customers** are often good bets. Some degree of uniqueness in these table names helps with monitoring, as you'll see later. Adding a company name in there,

---

[10] Once again, your passwords probably shouldn't taunt the attacker as I've done here. Make these accounts and their passwords look realistic. Taunting Duke basketball is always okay, though.

like **company_users** or even **companyusers**, also works. Leveraging the context of the web application helps too. For example, if you're running a popular content management system whose users table is often named **adm_users**, consider modifying the app to use an alternate table name. Now, give a honey table the name **adm_users**. When the attacker encounters your application, they'll look for that default users table and get the honey table instead.

Interactivity

While the honey table doesn't have to contain any data, it's kind of a missed opportunity if you leave it empty. Placing honey credentials in the honey table, as described in Chapter 8, helps provide another avenue for detecting the attacker and assessing their control on your network. Otherwise, the table will function as a typical database table and shouldn't need to provide additional interactivity beyond that.

Monitoring

While creating the honey table was straightforward, monitoring for access to it is a much more significant challenge. In an ideal world, MySQL provides the ability to audit queries to specific tables. However, the query logging functionality isn't that sophisticated and is mostly an all or nothing proposition. Logging every database query on a production server can add a tremendous amount of overhead. Even if you're not storing those logs, some estimates show that logging queries to a file can decrease server performance by 10-20%[11]. Nevertheless, it gets the job done (Figure 9-5).

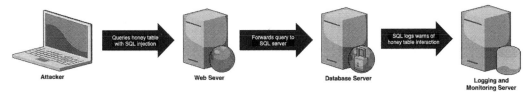

FIGURE 9-5:

Monitoring honey tables with MySQL general query logging

If you can afford the performance hit or just want to try this out yourself, enable MySQL's general query logging with these steps[12]:

---

[11] This article describes the various performance hits you'll see from general query logging https://www.fromdual.ch/general_query_log_vs_mysql_performance.

[12] These instructions will vary based on your version of MySQL. Get the instructions for your version by selecting it from the drop-down menu at https://dev.mysql.com/doc/refman/8.0/en/query-log.html.

1. Log in to the MySQL shell

```
sudo mysql -u username -p
```

2. Specify a file name for the log entries

```
SET GLOBAL general_log_file='query.log';
```

3. Enable the general log

```
SET GLOBAL general_log=1;
```

Now, you'll see log data like this in the file you specified (placed by default in **/var/log/ mysqld/**):

```
2020-05-28T17:53:02.320113Z          11 Query   SELECT * from company_
users
```

In this log entry, you see a SQL SELECT statement used to query the company_users honey table. Because any interaction with this table is abnormal, you'll want to alert on this event. Start with this SIGMA rule:

```
title: Honey Table Enumeration
description: Someone enumerated the contents of a honey table with the
SQL SELECT statement.
date: 2020/01/01
tags:
    - honeypot
author: Chris Sanders
logsource:
    product: mysql
    service: appdb
detection:
    selection:
        command: Query
        argument|contains|all:
            - SELECT
            - company_users
    condition: selection
fields:
    -  command
    -  argument
falsepositives:
    - Database backups
```

The MySQL general query log alone doesn't give you much information to start your investigation other than the query itself. However, you should be able to correlate the timestamp with other logs to build a more complete picture of the attack timeline. For example, web server access logs if that was the attack vector, or flow and PCAP data if the attacker came from elsewhere in the network.

The general query log grows quickly, so if you're attempting this technique in production you must ensure you rotate the log often and don't fill up the server's disk space. Pair this logging mechanism with egress filtering to only send the logs you want to a central log aggregator. If you're only logging this data for honeypot purposes, there's no need to keep it around on the server for long. You just need it there long enough for host-based detection tools to see the honey table access, or for log shippers to send the logs elsewhere for analysis and storage.

Since this logging mechanism doesn't have the granularity we'd like, general query logging might not be feasible for many due to the performance implications. There are a few other techniques you can try, but each has its own complexities and limitations.

Web Server Logs

Since many database compromises occur through misconfigured or insecurely developed web apps, you can rely on web server logs as an alternative means of providing alerts when attackers interact with honey tables. I showed you how to configure an Apache web server and access those logs in Chapter 7. That same configuration should capture the interaction with the database for some SQL injection techniques, but only those that appear as HTTP GET requests in the URL (Figure 9-6).

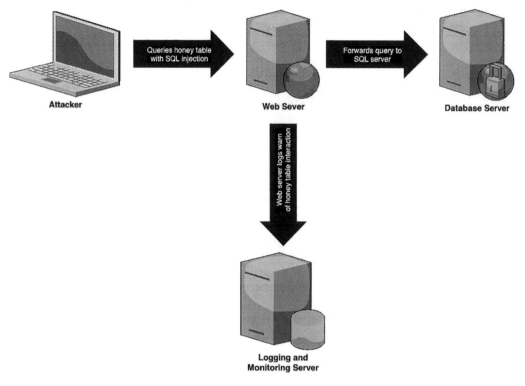

FIGURE 9-6:

Monitoring MySQL queries with web server logs

Look at the log below as an example:

```
10.100.94.12 - - [28/May/2020:16:11:53 +0000] "GET /app/
cart/?id=SELECT+username%2Cpassword+FROM+company_users+%3B&Submit=Submit
HTTP/1.1" 200 1773 "http://chrissanders.org/app/cart/" "Mozilla/5.0
(Macintosh; Intel Mac OS X 10_15_4) AppleWebKit/537.36 (KHTML, like
Gecko) Chrome/81.0.4044.138 Safari/537.36"
```

In this log entry, the attacker at 10.100.94.12 uses SQL injection to interact with the web app's backend database. Assuming this worked, a SQL SELECT query gives them the contents of the **company_users** honey table.

This SIGMA rule below detects some forms of SQL queries involving the honey table, including the log entry above. This rule isn't foolproof since SQL queries can manifest in different ways, so you'll want to experiment with different signature-based detection techniques. The good news is that any enumeration of the honey table is malicious, so you're less likely to encounter false positives if you use a somewhat unique (but still enticing) table name.

```
title: Honey Table Enumeration through Web Server
description: Someone enumerated the contents of a honey table through a
Web Server
date: 2020/01/01
tags:
    - honeypot
author: Chris Sanders
logsource:
    product: mysql
    service: appdb
detection:
    selection:
        request_line|contains:
            - 'company_users'
    condition: selection
fields:
    -   "Source IP"
    -   "User Agent"
    -   "HTTP Request"
level: high
```

Network Data

Attackers typically interact with database servers over the network. This interaction opens the door for network-based data monitoring techniques. For example, mirror the SQL server switch port to an interface connected to a network sensor running the Suricata IDS (Figure 9-7). This action gives Suricata the ability to observe network traffic to and from the SQL server, which should include database queries.

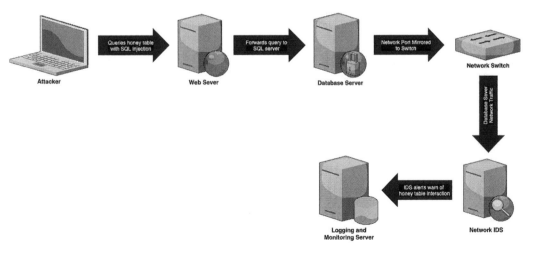

FIGURE 9-7:

Monitoring MySQL queries with Suricata

With Suricata's eyes on the queries, you're free to use network IDS rules to detect multiple variations of honey table enumeration. For example, this rule:

```
alert tcp any any -> $SQL_SERVER 3306 (msg:"Honey Table Enumeration";
flow:established,to_server; content:"company_users"; classtype:honeypot;
sid:50000001; rev:1;)
```

This signature alerts on a TCP connection from anywhere (**tcp any any**) to a designated SQL server on port 3306 (**$SQL_SERVER 3306**). This connection must be established to the server (**flow:established,to_server;**). The honey table name must be in the packet data (**content:"company_users";**).

This technique also isn't foolproof. For instance, if an attacker compromises the SQL server directly and runs queries on that system, the query data won't go across the network and you'll never see it. In this case, you'll hope that other detection mechanisms are present. Additionally, if the attacker issues commands to MySQL through an encrypted channel, Suricata won't be able to see the content of those queries unless you pair it with some mechanism allowing SSL/TLS man-in-the-middle.

MS SQL DNS Queries

While it only works on Microsoft SQL servers, the folks at Thinkst came up with a clever way to get this server to generate DNS queries when someone queries a specific table by using views (Figure 9-8). You can set the URL to whatever you like and monitor host or network DNS logs for evidence of these queries. When you see one, you know someone is accessing the honey table.

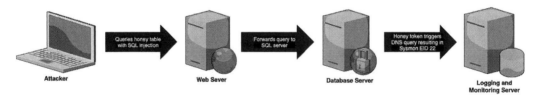

FIGURE 9-8:

Monitoring MS SQL queries with DNS logs

This technique is somewhat complicated and a bit difficult to understand without a great deal of SQL knowledge. Thinkst knows this too, which is why they set up an option to auto-generate a script that creates your own MS SQL view for use as a honey table at https://canarytokens.org. It relies on database triggers, which are functions called when executing certain types of SQL statements. If you want to dive into the guts of this technique, start by generating a script using the link above or examine the Canary Token source at: https://github.com/thinkst/canarytokens/blob/master/t-sql.txt/.

Once implemented, you'll monitor for DNS logs, as I described in the Honey Folder section of Chapter 7. If you're leveraging Sysmon DNS, this SIGMA rule detects the DNS query generated from browsing the table:

```
title: MS SQL Honey Table Access
description: Someone issued a query accessing an MS SQL honey table view
date: 2020/01/01
tags:
    - honeypot
author: Chris Sanders
logsource:
    product: windows
    service: sysmon
detection:
    selection:
        EventID: 22
        QueryName: '*%HONEYPOT_DOMAIN_HERE%'
    condition: selection
fields:
    -   QueryName
    -   Computer
falsepositives:
    - User Errors
level: high
```

If you're collecting DNS records from the network, this Suricata rule alerts when browsing a honey table generates a DNS query:

```
alert dns $HOME_NET any -> $EXTERNAL_DNS_SERVERS 53 (msg:"MS SQL Honey
Table Access"; dns.query; content:"%HONEYPOT_DOMAIN_HERE%"; nocase;
classtype:honeypot, sid:50000001; rev:1;)
```

Which of these monitoring techniques you use will depend on your existing monitoring tools, the database technology present in your network, and your comfort with the tradeoffs and limitations of each technique. Regardless, honey tables are a useful way to detect attackers operating close to sensitive information.

Honey Mailboxes

While I've geared most of the detection honeypots in this book towards monitoring network data and users, honeypots can have a role in monitoring concerns to individual privacy as well. Rob Graham's use of honey mailboxes provides a window into how this might work. Ahead of the 2016 US presidential election, Rob made a $10 donation to the campaign of every major candidate[13]. For each donation, he used a different email address. As expected, each address started receiving messages from the campaign to which it was tied. But then, something interesting happened. As candidates began to drop out of the race, accounts tied to one candidate started receiving messages from other campaigns. For example, when John Kasich dropped out of the race, that address began receiving messages from the Marco Rubio and John McCain campaigns. Not long after, Marco Rubio's designated account started receiving messages from the Ted Cruz and Rand Paul campaigns, along with campaigns tied to the U.S. House of Representatives races in Utah and South Carolina. Those tracking the data could see how it mirrored the shifting alliances of political endorsements. Perhaps more importantly to the individual donor, it shined a light on how organizations might abuse their stewardship of your personal information.

Building on this technique, you can create honey mailboxes to track how organizations protect the privacy of the account information you share with them.

---

[13] https://blog.erratasec.com/2015/09/i-gave-10-to-every-presidential.html.

SEE: The goal is for the organization to see a mail account and related.

 THINK: The organization should think that you're a legitimate human user signing up for whatever service or product they offer.

 DO: When the mail account starts receiving messages from someone other than the organization you tied it to, you'll know that they've shared your information, or someone stole it from them.

Configuring the Honeypot

The process of creating a honey mailbox is straightforward. Just pick an email provider and create a new account. The account should be unique for the organization, and you should only associate each account with one organization. Otherwise, you won't be sure which organization shared or lost your data when you do receive a message from a third party.

You'll usually have to supply more personal information with the registration than just an email address, which provides additional opportunity to understand what data was shared or lost. For example, let's say that you supply an organization with a unique first and last name and later receive a message from a third party that addresses you with that first and last name. Now, you know that name data was also included in whatever was shared or stolen.

How do you decide where you should use a honey mailbox? That, to many extents, depends on your threat model and goals. For example, let's say you're considering a partnership with another business and you're concerned about their diligence respecting user privacy. A honey mailbox provides a mechanism to see how they handle this data. In another scenario, imagine you live in a place where the government might be hostile or ambivalent towards certain parts of its citizenry. But, you still must utilize some government services, either by choice or by force. Knowing that facets of the government shared this email address with third parties might help you better understand or prepare for other threats you may face. Additionally, the flow of user data helps predict political or economic activity. For example, in some cases from the earlier political campaign example, supporters of political candidates saw messages from other candidates before theirs had dropped out of the race. Then, a few days later, their candidate dropped out and endorsed the third party they received messages from. The movement of data predicted the eventual public announcement. Finally, sometimes you just might be curious about a particular company or industry that you share your data with. That curiosity can help you find organizations that don't care as much about your privacy as you do, allowing you to spend your time or money with those that do.

Discoverability

Since you're submitting the address to organizations directly, you don't have to worry about them discovering it. However, you should take care to be sure other organizations or spam bots don't accidentally discover the address. That means it shouldn't be easily guessable based on a name and should have some degree of randomness.

Interactivity

Since you'll rely on incoming messages to monitor the account, it should be real. It's a good idea to host this on a third-party email provider rather than from your corporate mail server since there are scenarios where other attacks might expose user accounts and spoil the honeypot.

Monitoring

The process of monitoring honey accounts usually just means logging into those accounts and checking for new messages. However, that's tedious with more than a few accounts and it's easy to forget about it altogether. To help, I like to configure honey mailboxes to forward all incoming messages to one centralized account. Then, I leverage inbound mail rules to dump mail from each account into a folder. From there, I can also modify rules to forward messages not matching expected domains to a particular folder that I watch more closely. Let's walk through an example (Figure 9-9).

FIGURE 9-9:

Routing honey mailbox messages helps make monitoring more efficient

As part of accepting a new job, you've moved across the country to a new town. Because you have a chronic medical issue, you need to establish a new primary care physician. A coworker tells you about Dr. Burks, who comes highly rated. However, Dr. Burks works as part of a medical office associated with a big national hospital chain. Hospitals and medical offices have notoriously poor security practices in many cases, so you're worried that some of your data might be at risk. When you make your first visit, you decide to provide a honey mailbox address so you can track where your data goes.

First, you'll register a custom email account specifically for this medical office. Let's say that it's **chris_drb40195@gmail.com**[14]. Now, you can configure that account to forward all emails to another account so you don't have to log into it every time. In Gmail, accomplish this by browsing to **Settings**, **Forwarding and POP/IMAP**, and

---

[14] Some mail providers support adding tags to incoming mail by including the tag, followed by a plus (+) symbol, followed by the rest of your legitimate e-mail address. You might be tempted to try that here, but organizations often configure automated contact management systems to strip those tags, defeating their purpose.

clicking **Add a forwarding address** (Figure 9-10)[15]. You'll have to supply a code sent to the forwarding address to prove you have access to it.

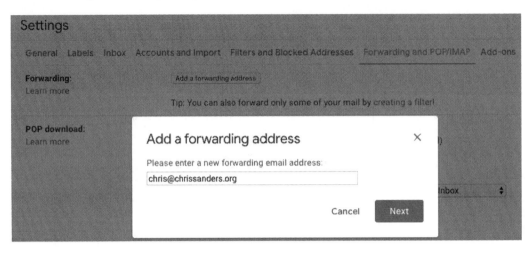

FIGURE 9-10:

Forwarding mail from a honey mailbox to a monitoring account

Now, you can set up custom message rules in your primary email account you'll use to monitor the honey mailbox. If you use Outlook to access a Microsoft Exchange mailbox, you'll follow this process:

1. In the main menu bar, click **File > New > Folder**. Name the folder *Honey Mailbox - Dr. Burks*. This folder is where you'll forward all messages to the honey mailbox. Next, repeat the process and create another new folder named *Honey Mailbox - Alerts*. This folder is where you'll forward third party messages to the honey mailbox.

2. Now, create the first rule—click **Tools** on the main menu and select **Rules**. Click Exchange under the Client Rules heading and click the plus symbol (+) to create a new rule. Configure the rules settings as I've done in Figure 9-11. This rule moves any mail sent to chris_drb40195@gmail.com into the Honey Mailbox—Dr. Burks folder.

---

[15] Forwarding with this technique is applied after spam filtering. If you want forward to apply to spam messages as well, you'll need to configure filtering rules in Gmail, which can also apply to spam.

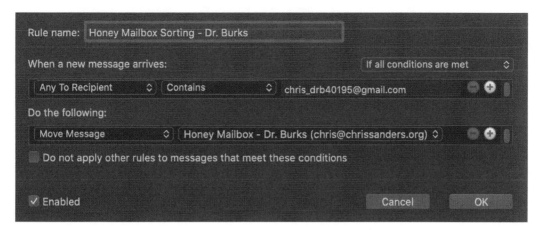

FIGURE 9-11:

Configuring the honey mailbox sorting rule

3. Repeat the process to create a new rule, matching the settings from Figure 9-12. This rule moves any mail sent to chris_drb40195@gmail.com but not from Dr. Burk's normal domain into the Honey Mailbox—Alerts folder. It also sets the priority of the message to Highest and plays a sound to catch your attention.

FIGURE 9-12:

Configuring the honey mailbox alerting rule

Now, if this account starts receiving loads of messages from insurance companies or medical device manufacturers, you'll know someone else has your data. That might be the product of the doctor's office or their parent hospital group selling the data or the result of an attacker targeting their patient databases that they may not know about or have disclosed yet.

While it's hard to ascertain which of the above scenarios might be closest to the truth, the examination of message headers can provide additional insight. Sometimes, organizations hire third-party companies to manage facets of their customer relationship management. These third parties may be the ones sharing your data. While you won't always be able to come to definite conclusions, similarities between the email headers of the primary organization and the third party, along with additional research, can reveal links between them. If you read these organizations' privacy policies carefully, you'll sometimes find them using specific language to skirt around what they can and can't do with your information. For example, just because an organization agrees not to sell your data doesn't mean they can't loan it away freely to existing business partners[16].

Lastly, consider extending honey mailbox monitoring to services like haveibeenpwned. com. This site aggregates data dumps from breaches that become public, and their free service lets you monitor for when an email account shows up in one of these dumps (Figure 9-13). If your honey account shows up in a dump, you'll know that the organization, someone affiliated with them, or someone they give your data to was breached.

---

[16] Rob's experiments found an example of how politicians were doing this, as well: https://blog. erratasec.com/2015/10/prez-rick-perry-selling-his-mailing-list.html.

Breaches you were pwned in

A "breach" is an incident where data has been unintentionally exposed to the public. Using the 1Password password manager helps you ensure all your passwords are strong and unique such that a breach of one service doesn't put your other services at risk.

Data Enrichment Exposure From PDL Customer: In October 2019, security researchers Vinny Troia and Bob Diachenko identified an unprotected Elasticsearch server holding 1.2 billion records of personal data. The exposed data included an index indicating it was sourced from data enrichment company People Data Labs (PDL) and contained 622 million unique email addresses. The server was not owned by PDL and it's believed a customer failed to properly secure the database. Exposed information included email addresses, phone numbers, social media profiles and job history data.

Compromised data: Email addresses, Employers, Geographic locations, Job titles, Names, Phone numbers, Social media profiles

You've Been Scraped: In October and November 2018, security researcher Bob Diachenko identified several unprotected MongoDB instances believed to be hosted by a data aggregator. Containing a total of over 66M records, the owner of the data couldn't be identified but it is believed to have been scraped from LinkedIn hence the title "You've Been Scraped". The exposed records included names, both work and personal email addresses, job titles and links to the individuals' LinkedIn profiles.

Compromised data: Email addresses, Employers, Geographic locations, Job titles, Names, Social media profiles

Data & Leads: In November 2018, security researcher Bob Diachenko identified an unprotected database believed to be hosted by a data aggregator. Upon further investigation, the data was linked to marketing company Data & Leads. The exposed Elasticsearch instance contained over 44M unique email addresses along with names, IP and physical addresses, phone numbers and employment information. No response was received from Data & Leads when contacted by Bob and their site subsequently went offline.

Compromised data: Email addresses, Employers, IP addresses, Job titles, Names, Phone numbers, Physical addresses

FIGURE 9-13:

This output from haveibeenpwned.com lists three places where a mail account was exposed publicly

Honey Commands

While attackers sometimes leverage malware and custom tools for post-compromise activities like establishing persistence and moving laterally, smart ones also rely on existing tools provided by the operating system. Because these tools serve legitimate purposes, security teams don't always monitor them closely and they don't risk the pitfall of being caught by antivirus or application allow-listing tools. Even more so, it's often just a lot simpler to use what's already there if it gets the job done. For example, attackers don't have to invest the time and effort to build their own custom persistence mechanism for a Linux system where crontab is available, which will run the attacker's tool at whatever schedule they set[17].

---

[17] And often, a lot more reliably.

An attacker's use of legitimate applications on systems, often called LOLBINs or LOLBAS[18], provide an opportunity to leverage honey tokens on Unix-based systems. With this technique, we'll create aliases for commonly used LOLBINs to include web bugs that alert us when attackers invoke them (Figure 9-14).

FIGURE 9-14:

When an attacker uses a LOLBIN on a Unix-based system, an alias invokes a honey token

 SEE: The goal is for the attacker to see a standard terminal with typical commands and tools available to them.

 THINK: The attacker should think the resident tools and commands function as they usually would.

 DO: When the attacker runs a honey command, the compromised system interacts with a web token letting us know the attacker is there.

Configuring the Honeypot

Before starting, know that you'll once again need a web server configured to receive requests from compromised systems transmitting honey tokens. I described the process of setting one of these up in the Honeydocs section of Chapter 7. For this example, you should deploy the web server inside your network perimeter. This placement is so that the logs show the actual local IP addresses of the hosts where attackers executed honey commands, which will also be inside the network perimeter.

Since we're going to bug a command by creating an alias for it, we'll start by identifying that command. In this case, we're going to target the wget tool, which retrieves content from web servers. While admins may run this tool legitimately, I wouldn't expect to see it much outside of initial system configuration or maintenance. Both, ideally, are things you can quickly verify are happening with a change management system or by speaking with the admin.

Now, let's create the alias. Typically, users create aliases for only their profile.

---

[18] Living Off the Land Binaries or Living Off the Land Binaries and Services

However, we want this alias to persist across every user. To do this, edit **/etc/bash.bashrc**. Then, place the alias in the file and save it[19]. We'll use this one:

```
alias wget='curl http://update.chrissanders.org/uk12 > /dev/null 2>&1 ;
wget'
```

Let's break this down step-by-step:

- **alias wget**: Defines the command for which the alias applies. Any time someone runs wget, the system executes what follows after the equals sign.
- **curl http://update.chrissanders.org/uk12**: Curl requests the URL that follows. In this case, the URL points to our honeypot web server. The uk12 portion of the request is a unique token explicitly created for this honeypot.
- **> /dev/null 2>&1**: Since we don't want the attacker to see the output of the curl command, it's sent to /dev/null. As an added layer, stderr is also disposed of in case the command fails.
- **; wget**: After all that, wget runs normally. Any URL or other parameters the attacker supplies are processed starting at this point. Since I used ; instead of &&, wget executes even if the first command fails.

The system won't apply the alias you created to active terminals immediately. To test it, you must either log out of your terminal session and start a new one or run the command **source /etc/bash.bashrc** to apply the changes at once. Now, whenever an attacker runs wget, they'll unknowingly fall into your trap and you'll soon know they're there.

Discoverability

Unix-based systems are most likely used on your network to run server infrastructure. That alone lends this to an inside-out strategy where you configure honey commands on servers close to sensitive data. While you won't specifically lure attackers here, the commands await them when they show up.

If you hope for attackers to invoke honey commands, you should plan to create aliases for the commands they are likely to use. For example, attackers often use the `tar` command to archive files for exfiltration, so that it might be a good candidate. However, you must also consider what legitimate commands admins are likely to run. At first

---

[19] There are several ways to implement aliases on a Unix-based system. Depending on the configuration of your system, you might need to leverage another strategy. The best breakdown of the most common mechanism I've found is here: https://askubuntu.com/questions/121413/understanding-bashrc-and-bash-profile/606882#606882.

thought, it might be useful to create an alias for the `ls` command that an attacker uses to list the contents of a directory. However, legitimate administrators will certainly also use this command, increasing the likelihood of false positives. It's probably not a good candidate for that reason. So, you must strike a balance, understanding which commands attackers are likely to use and how administrators use the server.

A few favorite targets of mine for honey commands are:

- **base64**: Attackers often use this tool to quickly scramble things they don't want to be picked up by network IDS signatures when transmitting data across the network.
- **tar**: As I mentioned above, attackers often archive data for exfiltration or moving the data to another system before exfiltration.
- **python**: While it's not generally a great idea to leave script interpreters on systems if you're not regularly running those types of scripts, creating aliases for these commands can catch attackers running malicious scripts.
- **vim**: If everyone else on the network uses nano to edit files[20], then detecting the use of other editors can be fruitful.

If you'd like a reasonably comprehensive list of LOLBINs that attackers might use on a Unix-based system, check out https://gtfobins.github.io/. This site also provides examples of how attackers commonly use each attack, which becomes helpful when investigating alerts from honey commands.

If you're working with a smaller team of systems administrators or running a network by yourself, you can get a little craftier here by creating alternative aliases for common commands. For example, I mentioned above that bugging the `ls` command would likely lead to many false positives since administrators use this command regularly. However, if you can get everyone on the same page, you can direct them to use an alternative command for which you've set up another alias. The line below, added to the bash.bashrc file created earlier, does that:

```
alias ls='curl http://update.chrissanders.org/uk12 > /dev/null 2>&1 ; ls'
alias altls='ls'
```

Now, whenever an administrator wants to use the `ls` functionality, they type **altls**. This alternative alias bypasses the honey command, which attackers are still likely to use when they run **ls**. This change can be challenging to get used to, so you might still accidentally generate several false positive alerts at first.

---

[20] As all sane, well-adjusted people do.

Interactivity

Ideally, the attacker experiences no interactivity beyond what the command they intend to run provides them already. By redirecting any stdout or stderr output away from the terminal, we've ensured they won't know they're running an alias. Of course, if the attacker compromises the system, then they could discover the changes to the bash.bashrc file and know that they've been duped. However, it's unlikely that they make this discovery before actually running some of those commands.

While I've only shown you how to connect a honey token web bug to commands by using an alias, you have the entire command shell at your disposal when the attacker executes a honey command. That means you can perform additional tricks that help you cause more interaction with the attacker or gather information about their tradecraft. For example, this alias invokes whoami to capture the user account executing the honey command and place it in the HTTP URL sent to the honeypot server receiving this request:

```
alias ls='curl http://update.chrissanders.org/uk12/$(whoami)/ > /dev/null
2>&1 ; ls'
```

Going farther, you could have the honey command execute a python script that collects relevant artifacts, archives them, and sends them to another system for analyst perusal when reviewing the alert. Be careful here, as you don't want the attacker noticing a time delay waiting for commands to run. To remedy this, you can run commands in parallel, rather than in sequence, as shown below:

```
alias wget='(python /etc/collect.py &) > /dev/null 2>&1 ; curl http://
update.chrissanders.org/uk12 > /dev/null 2>&1 ; wget'
```

In this example, we force the system to run a python script called collect.py whenever the attacker executes wget. By placing the single quotes (') around the command and adding the ampersand (**&**), the python script executes and runs in parallel with the other curl and wget commands. Because we don't want the attacker seeing output or errors from the script, stdout and stderr get redirected here as well. This redirection also hides the notification an attacker would otherwise see about the python process running in the background.

There's tremendous flexibility with this strategy. While I provided an example of how a Python script might collect investigative artifacts, you could do something more unique. Some examples include selectively placing additional context-appropriate interaction points in front of the attacker, manipulating responses to their commands, or redirecting them to a sandboxed environment.

Monitoring

Whenever an attacker runs a honey command, curl runs from that system and sends an HTTP request to the honeypot web server you configured to listen for honeypot interaction. The HTTP log generated from that request looks like this:

```
10.100.5.6 - - [01/Jun/2020:15:14:45 +0000] "GET /uk12 HTTP/1.1" 404 432
"-" "curl/7.58.0"
```

This log is similar to several other web bug examples I've demonstrated elsewhere in the book. The request comes from the system 10.100.5.6 where the attacker ran the honey command. The honey token is **uk12** and may identify some characteristics about the source depending on how you're organizing the tokens. Notably different from other examples is the user agent **curl/7.58.0**, which identifies the version of curl running on the system.

This SIGMA rule provides an alert when someone executes a honey command:

```
title: Honey Command Execution
description: Someone ran a honey command on an internal system.
date: 2020/01/01
tags:
    - honeypot
author: Chris Sanders
logsource:
    product: honeytoken
    service: honey_command
detection:
    selection:
        request_line|contains:
            - 'uk12'
            - 'token2'
            - 'token3'
    condition: selection
fields:
    -   "Source IP"
    -   "User Agent"
    -   "HTTP Request"
falsepositives:
    - Systems administrator
level: high
```

I recommend organizing honey tokens based on the command they're associated with since you won't otherwise have this data in the HTTP log entry. So, you'll use the same honey token for any aliased versions of wget, another honey token for aliased versions of tar, and so on. You'll know the system where the potential attacker executed the command based on the IP address in the HTTP log. Combined with knowing the executed command by virtue of the honey token, you'll have useful information to begin your investigation. I sometimes like to think of this configuration as a poor person's command line logging, but a version with the potential for greater efficacy when deployed thoughtfully.

Conclusion

In this chapter, I demonstrated more unique ways that honeypots manifest. Some of these were extensions of prior concepts like applying honey tokens to cloned websites, whereas others like honey tables don't fit neatly into just one of the primary categories. These techniques and others like them extend honeypots, providing more opportunities to find evil on your network.

AFTERWORD

WHAT IS A HONEYPOT?

If you've made it this far then you have a definition and several examples to help answer that question. However, I hope that through all these examples you've taken away a new mindset too. A honeypot isn't simply a piece of software, a specially configured system, or a decoy service. A honeypot represents the manifestation of deception-based detection. This is the idea that by controlling what the attacker sees, thinks, and does you can lure them into traps that let you know they're operating on your network.

I want to challenge you to start looking at your network with deception in mind. What assets are appealing to attackers? How can you mimic those assets? What breadcrumbs might lure attackers towards them? How will you know when attackers interact with them? These questions support your quest for a more cost-effective intrusion detection operation.

If you manage a small network, perhaps as an army of one or part of a small team, then start by implementing simple honey tokens from Chapter 7. They don't require much effort, ongoing maintenance, or additional logging infrastructure in many cases.

If you work on a larger team in an enterprise environment, thoughtfully consider the placement considerations in Chapter 3 and determine where honey services, systems, and credentials make sense given where common footholds and sensitive assets are located. Then implement your own versions of these honeypots while sending the alerts to your existing logging and monitoring infrastructure.

Once you start thinking about your network through the lens of defensive deception, it's hard not to see opportunities for the approach everywhere. The techniques in this book will help you get started, but they are by no means where you must stop. Although I only included about fifteen different honeypot techniques in this book, I came across dozens more in my research while writing it. The number grows tremendously when you consider the countless variations of simple service or token-based honeypots.

While honeypots have been around for a long time, I believe most organizations are still barely grasping their value and scratching the surface of the techniques available to them. With this book, you now have a roadmap for understanding and deploying honeypots that have a place in nearly every organization. With detection through deception, you can truly leverage home-field advantage. Be prepared for that opportunity.

Chris's Rosemary White Chocolate Pistachio Cookies

You might be asking yourself, "Self, why did Chris include a cookie recipe in a tech book?"

First, it's my book and I can do what I want here.

Second, finding evil is hard work. You should take time occasionally to recharge and treat yourself to something delicious. Better yet, make a batch and share it with coworkers in your SOC, NOC, or help desk. They'll appreciate the sentiment and their brains will appreciate the glucose.

Finally, I consider this an homage to Cliff Stoll's "The Cuckoo's Egg", which was the first book to ever mention honeypots. He included a recipe for chocolate chip cookies in his book. So, I'm carrying on the cookie torch. I hope whoever writes the next book about honeypots does the same.

Ingredients

This recipe makes around 20 cookies depending on how you size them on the pan. You can scale it up appropriately for larger batches, recognizing that your mixing bowl will be the limiting factor on batch size.

- Butter (Unsalted), 8 ounces
- All-Purpose Flour, 10 ounces
- Baking Soda, 3/4 tsp
- Kosher Salt, 2 tsp
- Vanilla Extract, 3 tsp
- Sugar, 4.5 ounces
- Eggs (Large), 2 Whole
- Light Brown Sugar, 5 ounces

- Molasses (preferably from fresh moles)[1], 2 tsp
- White Chocolate Chips, 8 ounces
- Whole Pistachios (rough chopped), 4 ounces
- Fresh Rosemary (minced, ideally fresh), 2 tsp

Procedure
Prep

1. Preheat your oven to 325 degrees.
2. Gather all the ingredients.
3. Shell and chop the pistachios, if necessary
4. Mince the rosemary

Process 1 - Brown Butter

5. Melt the butter in a saucepan on medium heat. Swirl it frequently until butter just begins turning brown and smelling nutty. Don't let it get too brown and burn.
6. Place the butter in a bowl in the fridge for half an hour to chill it back down.

Process 2 - Prepare Dry Mixture

7. In a bowl, mix together flour, baking soda, and salt.

Process 3 - Prepare Cookie Base

8. In a mixing bowl (a stand mixer bowl for less work), add sugar, eggs, and vanilla extract.
9. Mix vigorously until the mixture thickens and runs off a spoon in thick sheets. This should take about 3-5 minutes with a stand mixer. If you're doing this by hand, it will take a long time and you'll begin to hate life.

Process 4 - Add Components to Base

10. Add cooled brown butter and brown sugar to cookie base.
11. Add dry mixture to the cookie base. Mix slowly until just combined.
12. Add the chocolate, pistachio, and rosemary and mix for a few seconds until combined.
13. Put the dough in the fridge for an hour to chill the mixture.

Process 5 - Bake

14. Place parchment paper on a sheet pan.

---

[1] This is a joke. Don't harm any moles.

15. Roll 3 Tbsp of dough into a ball and place on sheet pan a few inches apart.

16. Bake for 13 minutes for a soft cookie (recommended) or 15 minutes for a crunchier one (if you hate joy). This will vary a bit based on your oven. Try doing a test cookie before doing the whole batch to get it perfect.

17. When finished, sprinkle a little salt over the top of the cookies and allow them to cool.

Enjoy!

INDEX

Page numbers with *n* indicate footnotes.

8/

Made in the USA
Monee, IL
14 October 2020